Catholic Evangelization
The Heart of
Ministry

Chris,
may God bless you!

Peace,

Rev. Robert J. Hater, Ph.D.

Bob Hater
6/3/04

Harcourt
Religion Publishers

Harcourt
Religion Publishers

Our Mission

The primary mission of Harcourt Religion Publishers is to provide the Catholic and Christian educational markets with the highest quality catechetical print and media resources. The content of these resources reflects the best insights of current theology, methodology, and pedagogical research. The resources are practical and easy to use, designed to meet expressed market needs, and written to reflect the teachings of the Catholic Church.

Nihil Obstat
Reverend Robert J. Hagedorn
Censor Librorum

Imprimatur
✠ Most Reverend Carl K. Moeddel
Auxiliary Bishop of the Archdiocese of Cincinnati
September 5, 2000

The Nihil Obstat and Imprimatur are official declarations that a book or pamphlet is free of doctrinal or moral error. No implication is contained therein that anyone who granted the Nihil Obstat and Imprimatur agree with the contents, opinions, or statements expressed.

Photo Credits
Corbis—Jeremy Horner: 33; Kit Kittle: 90; **FPG International**—Jill Sabella: 73;
SuperStock—145; Roderick Chen: 1; **Telegraph Herald**—53;
Tony Stone Images—Myrleen Cate: 125, 167

Printed in the United States of America

ISBN 0-15-901093-4

10   9   8   7   6   5   4   3   2

Dedications

I dedicated *News that is Good* to my mother with the words

Dedicated with love and gratitude to Olivia L. Hater, my mother, celebrating her 80th birthday, July 20, 1990. Mom's love strengthens me, her wisdom inspires me, her intelligence encourages me, and her faith gives me life.

I now rededicate *Catholic Evangelization: The Heart of Ministry* to my mother, Olivia L. Hater, celebrating her 90th birthday on July 20, 2000.

Mom, words cannot express my love for you. You bless me with your presence, love, and kindness. Your wisdom, intelligence, and courage inspire me. Your faith, hope, and positive attitude show me the way. The wonderful foods you make for me symbolize your love. Thanks for you and what you do for our family and me. God bless you! You are great!

I also dedicate this book to:

Steve and Babe Tenoever, my aunt and uncle. Your love and goodness to me since my childhood blessed me in so many ways. Sister Frances Hogan and Sister Helen Lacey. Your friendship and support over the years are deeply appreciated.

Contents

Introduction

Ten years have passed since I wrote *News that is Good: Evangelization for Catholics.* In that book, I began the Introduction with the words,

> "Spring's fresh air pours into my open window as I begin this work on evangelization. The chirping and singing of a robin outside promises new life and stimulates my recollections of family, God, Jesus, church and other faiths. It all seems fitting. After all, evangelization captures belief in God's presence, life's unity, human love, the Paschal mystery of Jesus, and the Christian community's concern for hurting people."

Now, I sit in the same room, but my eyesight is not as clear as it was then. One thing, however, becomes clearer. The Jesus, spoken of in *News that is Good,* is seen with greater clarity. God's all-pervasive presence becomes a living reality, as life merges into a more complete whole.

Catholic Evangelization: The Heart of Ministry relies heavily upon my first book, connecting original insights with ongoing developments in society and the Church. During the past ten years, the Catholic Church refocused itself on evangelization in a new way. It is now seen as central to Christian life and ministry.

The purpose of this book is to clarify the meaning of evangelization within the Catholic community, where the term sometimes still has negative connotations. Today, the Church sees evangelization as our invitation to share faith, and conversion as the "amen" to that invitation. For Catholics, this invitation to conversion is an ongoing process that invites us to enter ever more deeply into the mystery of God's love as manifested in the dying and rising of Jesus. Conversion happens as we say "yes" to God's message on many occasions during our lives. It is our lifelong journey with God.

Put in simplest terms, Catholic evangelization announces God's love through a faith commitment in our family, society, work place, and church. A parent's love, a neighbor's compassion, an employer's just business practices, an employee's work, a parish's welcome, and the witness of a good life are evangelization. All proclaim God's presence.

Catholic Evangelization: The Heart of Ministry aims at clarifying the meaning of evangelization for Catholics and encourages us to develop an evangelizing spirit. This book blends stories, pastoral insights, and theological wisdom into a practical synthesis. It is intended for anyone interested in Catholic life, pastoral practice, and teaching. In particular, this book is directed to: priests, pastoral ministers, and administrators, coordinators of Catholic evangelization, evangelization teams, directors of religious education, principals, teachers, catechists, renewal coordinators, RCIA directors, and anyone interested in sharing the good news of Jesus with others. Hopefully, the spiritual and pastoral approach that this book takes will help people realize more fully God's presence among us.

Since *News that is Good* was published, an explosion of interest in evangelization has occurred in Catholic circles, especially in Church documents. These writings reflect a consistency, centered in evangelization. The *General Directory for Catechesis* is especially noted. This document centers all ministries, especially catechetical ministry, within the dynamic of evangelization. Other important publications are progressively introduced throughout the book.

Catholic Evangelization: The Heart of Ministry is divided into ten chapters plus an appendix. Chapter one clarifies the meaning of Catholic evangelization, and chapter two stresses the connection between evangelization and the kingdom of God. Chapter three roots evangelization in the broader context of creation and life, which is the focal point of God's ongoing presence. Chapter four emphasized the close connection between evangelization and Christian spirituality, rooted in the kingdom of God. Chapter five studies evangelization and conversion. It considers the modes of God's presence, clarifies the meaning of conversion, looks at individual and communal conversion, and considers methods to help facilitate conversion.

Chapter six situates Catholic evangelization in the dialogue between the family, the world, and the parish. Chapter seven considers evangelization and ministry. Chapter eight looks holistically at how evangelization connects with the ministries of word, worship and service. An added opportunity for individual or group reflection on evangelization and Eucharist can be found in the appendix. This could be used after chapter eight or at any other point that it seems appropriate. Chapter nine reflects on evangelization implemented with a Catholic style. Chapter ten offers pastoral suggestions for evangelization in parish life.

Following each chapter, suggestions are offered for personal and pastoral reflection. These invite the reader to glean practical insights from the stories, pastoral message, and theological content of the chapter.

I hope this book helps carry out Jesus' call to proclaim God's love in our time. A robin's song, reverberating in my ears when I first prepared this manuscript, continues to reflect this love. May similar memories move us to recognize God's presence in our lives!

CHAPTER

1

CATHOLIC EVANGELIZATION
Meaning and Direction Today

Jim and Sally live in a small midwestern town. Now retired, they enjoy walking through shops, greeting old friends, and meeting new ones. One afternoon they saw a young woman walking alone. Recognizing her as a newcomer, they welcomed her. The woman's name was Connie.

Soon Connie, Jim and Sally sat in an ice cream parlor. Connie seemed so sad, so Jim and Sally invited her to their home. After a nice dinner and personal conversation, Connie expressed gratitude, and then told them she must leave.

On Holy Thursday, five years later, they received a package. Opening it up, Sally found a small frayed teddy bear and a letter, which read:

Dear Sally and Jim,

It's been a long time since we met. Remember five years ago when you bought me ice cream, invited me to your home for dinner, and listened to me? I was depressed but never told you why. The evening before, I learned I was pregnant. Unmarried and 19, I panicked, ran away, got off the bus in your town, and thought of killing myself. Your love, concern, and prayers changed my mind. When I left Jim said, "Trust God, and you will be okay." Those words, your kindness, and God's help saved my life. Enclosed find a small teddy bear. It is frayed and worn. This was my baby Erica's first toy. I want you to have it as a reminder that two people, myself and little Erica, owe you our lives. Thank you for giving us life. We are now fine. I pray that I can do for others what you have done for us.

Love,

Connie

Were Sally and Jim evangelizers? The answer is yes if we understand the term in light of the contemporary Catholic understanding of evangelization.

Before the Second Vatican Council, evangelization was not commonly used in Catholic pastoral practice or theology. Based on the thrust of this council, Pope Paul VI's apostolic exhortation, *Evangelization in the Modern World* (EN), set new directions for our understanding of evangelization.

Pope Paul stressed Jesus' life and ministry as the chief content of evangelization. Consequently, to appreciate evangelization, one looks to the New Testament, which reveals Jesus' evangelizing activities. In *Evangelization in the Modern World*, Pope Paul VI lists these activities as: Jesus' incarnation, his miracles and teachings, the gathering of the disciples, the sending out of the apostles, his crucifixion and resurrection, and the permanence of his presence in the Christian community. These remind us that evangelization is much more than words. It requires the active witness of faith, hope, and charity.

Pope Paul's emphasis moved Catholic scholars to look more deeply into the term evangelization. Jesus spoke Aramaic and probably used the word *sabar* for what subsequently was translated as *euangelizo* in the Greek New Testament. In Greek *euangelizo* means "to convey good news." The *Septuagint* or Greek translation of the Old Testament used this phrase in Samuel, Psalms, prophets, and the historical books. For example, Isaiah 52:7 refers to the good news that God has brought salvation.[1]

How beautiful upon the mountains
are the feet of the messenger who announces peace,
who brings good news,
who announces salvation,
who says to Zion, "Your God reigns."

---

[1]For a more detailed historical analysis of the terms evangelization and evangelism, see *Evangelize!: A Historical Survey of the Concept* by David Barrett, New Hope, Birmingham, Alabama, 1987. It was a helpful reference source for some of the historical materials in this section.

The early Christian Church used many other words for sharing the good news of salvation. For instance, St. John used the word *marturein* meaning "to give witness." *Keruxate*, meaning "to proclaim," was used also. This multiple use indicated that for the early Church sharing faith was *the* important thing. The words used to describe this activity were not as significant.

St. Paul used *euangelizo* to refer to Jesus' mission, ministry, life, and preaching. He also used it to indicate the activity of Christians when proclaiming Jesus' good news to non-believers. Early Christian writers, like Clement of Rome, Justin Martyr, Irenaeus, John Chrysostom and others used the Greek word *euangelizo*. When Latin became prominent in Western Christianity, this word was translated, *evangelizo*. This term was used by St. Thomas and others after him.

Through the Middle Ages *evangelizo* was translated into Old English and gradually into Modern English. John Wycliffe, Francis Bacon, Thomas Hobbes, and other scholars and religious figures employed it. Gradually, the term took two forms in English, *evangelism* and *evangelization.*

During the nineteenth century, *evangelism* began to be used by some Protestant Churches, but no such term was used in the Catholic community. This changed in 1956 when Cardinal Suenens in the *Gospel to Every Creature* linked evangelization to the entire Christian endeavor. This book included a preface by the future Pope Paul VI, whose *Evangelization in the Modern World* revolutionized the Catholic use of the word evangelization. Today the word evangelization, not evangelism, is employed in Catholic ministry to refer to sharing the good news of God's love. Although its focus differs from the past, evangelization is a new way to refer to an old reality, namely, the invitation for Catholics to share their faith.

Before this holistic view of evangelization came into focus, a more restricted approach was popular in some Catholic quarters. It saw evangelization and pre-evangelization as operative before a person makes a faith commitment. This approach was used in the 1960s and 1970s, especially in catechetical and missionary work. Some Catholics, active in the Church's pastoral ministries during these years, still understand evangelization in this way today.

The following model illustrates this older approach:

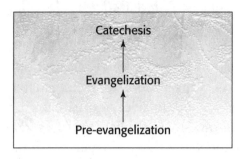

Catechesis

↑

Evangelization

↑

Pre-evangelization

Pre-evangelization, which sets the stage for evangelization, includes welcome, kindness, charity, and social concern that prepare people to receive God's word. Once the climate is set, evangelization helps people learn about Jesus and the Church. As evangelization proceeds, and people look toward a faith commitment, catechesis begins.

This threefold movement is hinted at in the *Rite of Christian Initiation of Adults* (RCIA). Here, pre-evangelization and evangelization are operative in the pre-catechumenal stage. When the person chooses to become a catechumen, catechesis starts. Hence, evangelization is seen in terms of the initial proclamation of the gospel, which is directed toward conversion and is followed by catechesis. In this approach, people are evangelized before and catechized after they make an initial faith commitment.

This view of evangelization emphasizes the importance of setting a proper climate for God's word and acknowledging a person's level of readiness. It becomes problematic, however, if it dichotomizes evangelization and catechesis, which are not an either/or; namely, first evangelization, then catechesis. Rather, as the holistic approach says, catechesis is an aspect or moment in the evangelization process (*On Catechesis in Our Time*, #18).

Since Pope Paul's *Evangelization in the Modern World* (1975), subsequent Church documents have clarified the new direction initiated by Pope Paul. Pope John Paul II stressed that catechesis is an aspect of the evangelization process in *On Catechesis in Our Time* (1978). In *On the Permanent Validity of the Church's Missionary Mandate* (1990), Pope John Paul II connects evangelization with the Church's missionary mandate. The United States bishops applied the new directions to this country in *Go and Make Disciples: A Plan and Strategy for Catholic Evangelization in the United States* (1993) and in *Thy Kingdom Come* (1999).

The *General Directory for Catechesis* (GDC) (1998) solidified and focused the developing notions of evangelization since Vatican II. This document sees evangelization as the thread that weaves through all Church ministries and the lives of Christians in the world.

In simplest terms, the Catholic Church holds that evangelization is the heart and soul of the Christian life. It happens whenever a Christian shares, directly or indirectly, Jesus' good news.

Among most Catholics, this holistic view of evangelization is not widely understood. This came home recently when I taught an upper-level undergraduate ministry class on evangelization. I asked the students their reaction to the word *evangelization.*

Their responses, mostly negative, surprised me. The vast majority associated it with fundamentalism, especially the preaching of televangelists. "Why talk about evangelization in a class on Catholic ministry?" asked one student. "Is that what we are about?" Most students had no idea what evangelization meant.

Because evangelization is widely misunderstood, it is important to clarify its meaning. This clarification sees evangelization as the energizing spirit of all Church ministries and the Christian's life in the family and world. A preparatory document for the 1973 World Synod on Evangelization describes it as "the activity whereby the Church proclaims the gospel, so that the faith may be aroused, may unfold, and may grow" (pages 1–2). Pope Paul VI in *Evangelization in the Modern World* (EN) states, "For the Church, to evangelize means bringing the Good News into all strata of humanity, and through its influence, transforming humanity from within and making it new" (#18).

The *General Directory for Catechesis* emphasizes that evangelization happens through words and deeds. It is "at once testimony and proclamation, word and sacrament, teaching and task" (#39). The Directory continues, "Proclamation, witness, teaching, sacraments, love of neighbor: all of these aspects are the means by which the one Gospel is transmitted and they constitute the essential elements of evangelization itself" (#46).

Evangelization embraces all aspects of a Christian's life. Seen in this way, *evangelization is a process fostering ongoing conversion within the Christian community that seeks to initiate people ever more deeply into the mystery of God's love (the kingdom), as it is manifested most fully in the dying and rising of Jesus.* (Hope)

Evangelization is the invitation to accept the good news of God's love. Evidence of God's love, which first comes from life itself and sets the stage for Jesus' revelation, can be referred to as *implicit* evangelization. Examples include the beauty of creation, the love from a parent, the compassionate listening of a friend, or the community life of a parish. Even if Jesus' name is not mentioned, evangelization happens in implicit ways, thus preparing for more explicit manifestations of Jesus' saving word.

Explicit evangelization proclaims the role of Jesus, God, kingdom, and Church in God's plan of salvation and gives deeper insights into the God already present in implicit evangelization. This happens formally in a church, classroom, or study group; and informally when alone, with friends, or in the workplace. Christians respond to explicit proclamation through service, and celebrate it through worship and prayer. Implicit and explicit evangelization foster ongoing conversion.

Conversion happens between God and individuals within a Christian community. Conversion is always communitarian, for we learn our deepest values from others. Even when conversion occurs in solitary moments, it happens because we live in a family, communicate with friends, work with associates, and worship with others people who influence us.

Evangelization seeks to initiate people deeply into the mystery of God's love. This initiation requires explicit proclamation of the gospel. Recently, a friend told me that after an accident he tried to discover how God was speaking to him through his injuries. The crucifix was the only symbol that gave him hope and a reason to go on. As he grew to appreciate how it connected with his suffering, the Scriptures took on new meaning. Reading the story of Christ's passion, meditating on the crucifix, and celebrating the Eucharist evangelized him in ways that nature or a friend's love hadn't.

Evangelization reveals that God's love is manifested most fully in the death and resurrection of Jesus. During my friend's sickness, he learned how Jesus' death reflected God's love. Soren Kierkegaard describes this love, climaxed on the cross, as "the supreme paradox." A God dying for creatures makes no sense but through faith this act is seen as a source of salvation. Jesus being raised from the dead by the Father is the final testimony, affirming that no matter what conclusions we draw from suffering, disappointment, or frustration, Christian faith says God's love transcends death and promises eventual happiness.

Evangelization, a life-long process, is a response to God's call to proclaim the good news of the kingdom in word and deed. It is not a separate ministry but is central to all ministries (GDC #46). Evangelization is the heart of ongoing conversion, in which God's word doesn't change, but our ability to hear it changes, depending on our age and circumstances. This understanding differs from the evangelism of the fundamentalists, which emphasizes hearing God's word and accepting Jesus Christ once and for all in a definitive moment of conversion and salvation.

The risen Lord evangelizes through the Christian community. For the Church, evangelization means "first of all to bear witness, in a simple and direct way, to God revealed by Jesus Christ, in the Holy Spirit; to bear witness that in his Son God has loved the world—that in his incarnate Word he has given being to all things and has called men to eternal life" (EN #26). Consequently, evangelization means that people hear the good news of God's forgiveness because we forgive; that people see Christian hope because they witness our hope; and that people celebrate divine friendship because we dare to be friends.

In the evangelization process the living Lord is experienced in flesh and blood—in the joys and tears of everyday life because we are bold enough to live as if God is our loving Father. Evangelical witness "will always contain as the foundation, center, and at the same time summit of its dynamism—a clear proclamation that, in Jesus Christ, the Son of God made man, who died and rose from the dead, salvation is offered to all men, as a gift of God's grace and mercy" (EN #27).

Evangelization is the kingdom in action, telling society that the word of Jesus is alive. Every day, family members proclaim God's word to one another through patience, sacrifice, and generosity. Workers and managers proclaim God's word in the workplace by following gospel values of justice and fairness. Churches support and assist members through preaching, teaching, liturgy, counseling, and generous giving to the marginalized.

Evangelization is the lifeblood of Christian life and ministry. As an ongoing activity of the Christian community, it includes the initial proclamation of the word, as well as the various pastoral ministries that nourish this initial proclamation. The *General Directory for Catechesis* describes three necessary moments in the process of evangelization. They are missionary activity to proclaim the good news to those who do not believe, initial catechesis for those who believe in Jesus and seek to deepen their process of initiation into the faith, and pastoral activity directed to strengthening the faith of believers (GDC #49).

Evangelization receives further specification in the ministries of word, worship and service. Consequently, evangelization happens in catechesis and preaching, prayer and liturgy, and service. The following diagram of the evangelization tree focuses the new Catholic evangelization.

This approach to evangelization is holistic, where the various ministries converge into a totality. (NCCE Fourth Annual Conference Proceedings, 1987 and GDC #46) The whole tree represents the evangelization process with three chief aspects: word, worship and service. Evangelization, while rooted in nature and life, takes its nourishment from God's Spirit.

In proclaiming the lived reality of Jesus' dying, rising, and sending of the Spirit, evangelization energizes Christian efforts, reminding us of our mission to live God's kingdom. Christian life is rooted in the lifeblood and marrow of evangelization. Without it, individual or institutional efforts to proclaim God's Word, celebrate it and serve others lack the dynamism promised by Jesus' good news.

Catholic Evangelization: Meaning and Direction Today

Personal and Pastoral Reflections

Appreciating the new evangelization means seeing it in a positive sense. For some people this requires clarification of the term, how it fits into the Catholic tradition, and why it is used today. For others, it means changing one's attitude from a negative one, closely associated with an evangelical or fundamentalist approach, to a holistic Catholic one.

To assist this process, we will consider key notions raised in this chapter. These can be studied individually or discussed with family members, school groups, or parish education meetings. The insights derived from such reflections provide fodder for further discussion or actions within the family, among friends, in the parish, or neighborhood.

1. **Clarifying the meaning of evangelization, as used in the Catholic Church**
   a. If someone asked you to describe evangelization in the Catholic Church, what would be your response?
   b. What points in this chapter helped you clarify its meaning?
   c. Do mainline Protestant Churches use the term *evangelization* or *evangelism*, in a similar way as Catholics use it? Discuss.

2. **Implications of Catholic Evangelization for family life, work, and parish ministry.**
   a. What consequences can Catholic evangelization have on the approach you take to your family life?
   b. How does a greater appreciation of Catholic evangelization help you see more clearly the role of the lay person in the world, neighborhood, and marketplace? Why?
   c. How could you do missionary work in your own country, neighborhood, or family?
   d. What would the implications be for you if came to see that evangelization is a new word for an old reality?

e. In what ways have Catholics always shared the good news of God's love, even if we did not use the word evangelization?

3. **Action Steps**

   a. Take practical steps to apply insights gleaned from this chapter to your family, neighborhood, and personal life.

   b. Discuss with a parish group or friends how the contents of this chapter can help the parish. If specific suggestions surface, convey them to the parish leadership.

   c. Establish a Catholic evangelization study and action group in your neighborhood or parish. Once set up, study Church documents on evangelization and pray with the Scriptures, asking God to give you guidance in your evangelization efforts.

   d. Encourage the pastor and pastoral leadership to clarify the meaning of Catholic evangelization for parishioners, through adult education sessions, parish meetings, catechetical activities, social ministry, and liturgy.

CHAPTER

2

EVANGELIZATION, KINGDOM, AND DISCIPLESHIP

Word came to a downtown parish that Millie, a bag lady, died. She had requested a Catholic burial. Shortly before the funeral liturgy began, the priest heard noise in the church. Looking out from the sacristy, he saw beggars, alcoholics, bag ladies, and other street people assembling for the service. The church was filled.

Unable to explain what was happening, the priest discarded his prepared homily, and instead walked among the congregation, and said, "Welcome! Why are all of you here? Who was this woman?"

A beggar responded, "Millie was the kindest person I knew. I loved her. She was good to me." An alcoholic continued, "That's right; she taught me about Jesus and gave me her coat when I was cold." The bag ladies nodded in approval. They all loved Millie, the "Saint of the Streets." That's why they came.

Street people knew Millie, even if parish ministers did not. Sharing her possessions with the poor spoke to them of God.

Millie's story recalls the episode in the Nazareth synagogue when Jesus said, "The Spirit of the Lord is upon me, because he has anointed me to bring good news to the poor. He has sent me to proclaim release to the captives and recovery of sight to the blind, to let the oppressed go free, to proclaim the year of the Lord's favor" (Luke 4:18–19). Jesus' words are the heart of the kingdom, which is the goal of evangelization. What then is the kingdom of God that Jesus proclaimed?

The biblical terms for kingdom—*malkuth* in Hebrew and *basileia* in Greek—are sometimes translated into English as *reign* or *rule* because *kingdom* has a male orientation. But these translations fail to capture the full impact of the biblical use of the word *kingdom*.

The Hebrew and Greek words imply the power symbolized by a strong ruler or king. Such power meant the submission of a servant to a master. Jesus turned this definition of power on its head by applying a paradoxical twist to its meaning. For the follower of Christ, power means service. He said, "You call me Teacher and Lord—and you are right, for that is what I am. So if I, your Lord and Teacher, have washed your feet, you also ought to wash one another's feet" (John 13:13–14).

Kingdom does not imply king in the sense that it gives precedence to a male figure. It refers to man and woman in equal measure. When using the word *kingdom*, the Christian dares to serve and to accept as Jesus did the total equality of man and woman, young and old, servant and master. As St. Paul says in Galatians, "There is no longer Jew or Greek, there is no longer slave or free, there is no longer male and female; for all of you are one in Christ Jesus" (Galatians 3:28).

It helps us to translate kingdom as *presence.* Both the Old and New Testaments describe this presence as freeing people from brokenness and sin and moving them toward health and wholeness. The goal of the kingdom is to give life and freedom, not death and bondage.

Jesus and the Kingdom

The kingdom of God is the key with which to understand Jesus' mission and to appreciate Catholic evangelization (GDC #34). A personal experience helped me see the kingdom of God in a contemporary focus.

Ben spent much of his time ministering to poor people. He resided in a two-room apartment in the inner city, surviving without a full-time salary or benefits. He had an old truck and tremendous faith in God.

He called me two weeks before Christmas, saying that the poor in Appalachia were in particularly difficult condition this year, because the government cut back certain assistance programs. He asked me to get him food, clothes, and blankets to fill his truck so he could help them this Christmas. I obtained the items he requested.

Several days after Christmas, we planned to go out for lunch. I met him at his apartment. His austere surroundings struck me. With his simple mountain furniture, it was almost as if a mountain cabin had been moved to the city. While looking around, my eyes settled on several black and white photographs hanging on the wall. The center one showed three poorly dressed women, several children, some chickens, and a dog standing in the dirt before a large, rusted tin shed. The shed was about thirty feet long, fifteen feet deep, and eight feet high. It protruded from a mountain, which formed the back wall.

"Who are those women and where is that shed?" I asked. Ben replied, "That's where we celebrated Christmas this year. Inside the shed, I gave out the supplies you obtained for me. The old woman in the middle lived in a cave until three years ago. The other women and children were abandoned. They got together and started living in the shed which the coal companies once used for storage."

Ben continued. "I want you to hear something." He picked up an old tape recorder and located the place he wanted on the tape. "This," he said, "is from our Christmas celebration in the tin shed." I listened. The guitar was a bit flat and the singers off-key, but from that tape came joy, peace, and love like I have never experienced on any professionally produced tape. Then it struck me, "This must have been the way it was the night Jesus was born!"

He came among the poor in an out-of-the-way place. His first visitors were shepherds, who often had reputations as thieves. Sometimes they took food and other necessities to support themselves and their families. Together, like the poor of the Gospels, the Appalachian poor celebrated God's love and renewed their hope by living again the story of Jesus' birth.

Then something else hit me. For the first time, I realized that the stories describing Jesus' birth and early life were written to introduce a key theme at the heart of the Gospels—the kingdom of God. These stories are introductions to Jesus' kingdom message. They tell how Jesus was rejected, cast out, and broken not only in his last days, but also from the beginning of his life.

Jesus accepted an impoverished state to show us the depth of God's love. Because Jesus—who is God—accepted the human brokenness that Scripture describes, we have confidence that God is in the hurting, broken conditions of every one of us. The Christian God is a God who loves everyone, but is present especially when we are hurting and broken, helping us become whole and holy.

Today, as in Jesus' time, many hurting people struggle to survive. Their brokenness may be economic, psychological, spiritual, or physical. Whatever the brokenness, human stories of pain and grief offer an invitation to reflect on God's love for every person.

Christians are the bearers of Jesus' good news. In so doing, we embody the relationship between evangelization and the kingdom, reflected in Pope Paul VI's words, "There is no true evangelization if the name, the teaching, the life, the promises, the kingdom, and the mystery of Jesus of Nazareth, the Son of God are not proclaimed" (EN, #22). In relation to these words, *Go And Make Disciples* (GMD) says, "We can understand evangelization in light of these stories of faith: namely, how we have been changed by the power of Christ's word and sacraments, and how we have an essential role in sharing that faith through our daily lives as believers" (GMD, page 10).

To better appreciate the meaning of the word *kingdom*, Scripture reminds us of the following:

- God sent Jesus.
- He knew poverty.
- His mission was to proclaim the kingdom of God.
- He did this through his ministry: namely, his life, words, and deeds.
- The kingdom is directed toward the poor, whether they are experiencing economic, physical, psychological, or spiritual poverty.
- The kingdom brings healing, reconciliation, and forgiveness.

The poor were a special focus of Jesus' ministry. He proclaimed good news to the poor, salvation to sinners, and hope to those without hope. In becoming one like us, Jesus was born in poverty and experienced forms of economic, physical, psychological, and spiritual poverty.

Jesus taught us that poverty is an evil to be overcome, not a condition to be maintained. Therefore, while God is a friend of the poor, this same God calls us to root out poverty. Jesus gives testimony to God's plan in becoming one like us in everything, except sin.

Jesus was born in *economic poverty,* far from city affluence and comfort. In his adult years as a wandering preacher, he was not bound to material possessions, saying of himself, ". . .the Son of Man has nowhere to lay his head" (Matthew 8:20).

Jesus also accepted *physical poverty,* which implies bodily suffering. The stories of his birth hint at the pain Jesus experienced in the difficult situation of his birth. Jesus' agony and crucifixion are supreme symbols of his willingness to embrace physical poverty.

Jesus' *psychological poverty* must have been intense. Throughout his life, people misunderstood him. They threw him out of the

Temple, opposed his teaching, harassed his disciples, and accused him of blasphemy. Judas betrayed him and Peter denied him. Jesus agonized in the garden and cried out on the cross. Psychological or emotional poverty permeated his life.

Jesus was not exempt from *spiritual poverty*. He was without sin which saved him from one form of spiritual poverty. He accepted, however, the condition of human loneliness and alienation to save the world. Lack of meaning is also a form of spiritual poverty. Consciousness of his mission gave meaning to Jesus' life. But when near death, he questioned the meaning of what was happening to him, when he cried out, "My God, my God, why have you forsaken me?" (Mark 15:34). Jesus' rejection and isolation lead to questions like the one he uttered to his Father. But when despair tempted him, he turned to God, saying, "Father, into your hands I command my spirit" (Luke 23:46).

The Gospels indicate clearly that Jesus assumed the human condition. God's presence, reflected in Jesus' teaching on the kingdom, was central to his life and ministry. He became poor to vanquish poverty. His example affords hope for anyone immersed in poverty, for Jesus teaches that poverty is never the end.

Healing, reconciliation, and forgiveness are the results of the presence of God's kingdom. When these happen, God is there. To learn to what degree a parish, school, family, or individual lives the kingdom message, one might observe their willingness to reconcile or forgive.

Jesus says to the Pharisees, "Which is easier to say, 'Your sins are forgiven you,' or to say, 'Stand up and walk'? But so you may know that the Son of Man has authority on earth to forgive sins" he said to the paralyzed man, "I order you: get up, and pick up your stretcher and go home" (Luke 5:23–24).

Reconciliation always brings miracles, for whenever life's broken pieces are mended, peace follows. A miracle happens when we say *amen* to urgings of our God—always-present and encouraging us to forgive. We begin to put the pieces back together.

The word *reconciliation*, when used generically, means "putting the pieces back together to establish peace." Closely associated with healing, reconciliation can happen in economic, physical, psychological, and spiritual poverty as individuals and groups are healed. Sometimes, this implies reconciliation with oneself after making a mistake. At other times, it means reconciliation with another. It also refers to reconciliation with God. Usually being reconciled with self, others, and God happens together.

Forgiveness, one form of reconciliation, may be necessary because of misunderstandings, mistakes, or sin. Jesus' resurrection is the supreme sign of reconciliation with God through the forgiveness of sin. God raised Jesus from the dead as a final testimony of his mission and ministry to lead us away from sin and toward salvation. The early Christians realized the significance of reconciliation more clearly after Jesus' resurrection. This realization enabled them to include in the New Testament many testimonies to the power of forgiveness.

Jesus' miracles symbolize God's desire to overcome poverty and brokenness. Miracles do happen. People don't cause them, God does. But people aid in God's creative desire to make all things whole. Reconciliation implies any efforts, including miracles, that bring wholeness to an individual or group. The Gospels describe Jesus' healing, reconciling ministry in stories such as the man born blind, Peter's mother-in-law, and Zacchaeus. In each instance, new life enters a person when healing occurs.

Reconciliation, because it includes forgiveness, is not easy. While on earth, we dwell in the kingdom of the "now," where God's presence with imperfect people helps us become whole. This takes time. Often I can only say, "God, help me become whole, I hurt so much," or "God, help me repair my broken marriage or friendship," or "God, help me be reconciled with my child."

Only in heaven will healing, reconciliation, and forgiveness be complete. Then there will be no more suffering, no more pain, no more hurt.

Church and the Kingdom of God

Jesus' mission and ministry continues in his earthly body, the Church. This realization dawned on the disciples at Pentecost as the Holy Spirit illuminated them helping them see how the Christian community is the body of Christ, responsible to proclaim the kingdom under the guidance of the Spirit. The Church does this through its corporate and individual ministry of teaching, good example, worship, prayer, and social concern. As *On the Vocation and Mission of the Lay Faithful in the Church and in the World* states, "Without doubt the Church has the Kingdom of God as her supreme goal, of which 'she on earth is its seed and beginning' (*Lumen Gentium*, 5) and is therefore totally consecrated to the glorification of the Father" (CL, #36).

The Church brings God's kingdom to completion. As John Paul II says in *On the Permanent Validity of the Church's Missionary Mandate*, "Likewise, one may not separate the kingdom from the Church. It is true that the Church is not an end unto herself, since she is ordered toward the kingdom of God of which she is the seed, sign, and instrument" (RM, #18). Like the life of Jesus, the Church is directed toward the poor and broken, offering them healing, reconciliation, and forgiveness. The spirit of the kingdom of God, so powerfully preserved in the Beatitudes and the Sermon on the Mount, continues to inspire us to follow Jesus as disciples (Matthew 5:3–12) (CCC, #1716). Like Jesus, the Church brings the kingdom to those who are economically, physically, psychologically, or spiritually poor. These conditions take distinct forms today.

Much of the world is *economically impoverished* as millions of people, lacking adequate food, clothing, and shelter, are left to a cruel fate. Some Christians help them by giving money and goods to the poor or by volunteering their services. This kind of giving, good and necessary in itself, aids many people. But it can subtly camouflage real poverty issues, for charity will never alleviate poverty; only justice will.

More and more Christians are accepting the kingdom's call to work for justice and oppose the economic, social, and political systems that keep people impoverished. The presence of God calls Christian political leaders, business executives, workers, and family members to carry out their mission to help alleviate economic poverty. The United States bishops in *Sharing Catholic Social Teaching: Challenges and Directions* spoke of this obligation in these words, "We believe that every person is precious, that people are more important than things, and that the measure of every institution is whether it threatens or enhances the life and dignity of the human person" (page 4).

Physical poverty refers to bodily impairments caused by such things as sickness, accidents, handicaps of birth, or the aging process. The Gospels recount many stories of Jesus healing those who suffered from physical poverty. The kingdom proclaimed by Jesus' life and ministry promises God's presence through his Church to those suffering from physical poverty.

Marcia is a dormitory placement coordinator at a large university. Seven students came to her office the first day of the fall semester demanding to be moved from the dormitory where they were assigned. "Why?" Marcia inquired. Bill, a strong, athletic man, spoke for the group. "The people there are different. Some don't speak right, others can't walk, still others are hunched over." Marcia realized immediately that the students had been assigned to the dormitory for the persons with disabilities.

She told them she would get their rooms changed, but it would take about a month. Sue, one of the seven students, was adamant, saying, "We want out now!" Finally, the group reluctantly agreed to stay in this dorm until changes could be arranged. They were to check back later with Marcia.

About three weeks later, Marcia was eating dinner in a popular restaurant. She heard laughing and hilarity in an adjoining room. Looking through the door, she saw the seven students who came to her office. Sue was helping a girl with a disability cut her food. Another assisted a young man with his vegetables. After some time,

Bill raised a glass and said, "Let's toast God for bringing us together." Then, turning to a severely disabled student, he said, "Happy Birthday, Ed!"

Marcia waited for the students to return to her office. One month passed, then a few more, and finally the year ended. They never returned to change their dormitory. These students learned from the gospel message, "Blessed are the poor in spirit" (Matthew 5:3). The physically disabled students taught the other seven about life.

Catholic evangelizers can learn valuable lessons from this story. When reaching out to help, more than the persons with the disability are blessed.

Psychological poverty is also widespread in modern society. Life's fast pace, the pressures to balance work and family life, the widespread use of drugs, divorce, and other social ills drive people to emotional upheaval and illness. Too often, life becomes a series of chores to be fulfilled rather than an exciting mystery to be celebrated.

Some years ago, a college student responded negatively to my efforts to help him in class. During the first four weeks, he missed many classes and most assignments. When I asked him why, he said, "I'm not interested in this class. I took it because I have to. After school, I work to pay for my education. This takes too much of my time." Halfway through the term, I talked to him again. By this time, he was doing even less work and rarely came to class. I told him I couldn't pass him unless he improved. He became adamant and said he didn't care.

Finally, I threw my grade book on the desk and said, "Bill, I don't care about your grades, but I do care about you. Won't you please let me be your friend?" Hearing this, this large young man fell on me and sobbed like a baby. Finally, he looked up and said, "Father, you are the first person in my life that ever asked me to be his friend." He never missed another class, made up his work, and got a "B."

Bill suffered from a gnawing loneliness that paralyzed him in an almost meaningless life. He needed encouragement and a friend. There are many people like Bill. They invite us to reach out to them. Evangelization gives this kind of witness to help further God's kingdom.

People who suffer from mental breakdowns or who have developmental disabilities also experience psychological poverty. These individuals need understanding but also invite us to gain a deeper understanding of the gospel message.

Years ago, a twenty-eight year old priest, Joe, had a mental breakdown while serving in the missions. This once athletic, humorous, brilliant man was never again the same. He tried several assignments over the years, but was unable to function. Eventually, he returned to the monastery, where he offered daily Mass, prayed, and walked the streets of the town talking to people.

When Joe died, his family and members of his order were amazed as hundreds of people filled the church, most of them unknown, poor, and ordinary. After the funeral, the family discovered that Joe was a spiritual advisor for many people in the town near his monastery. He did more than just greet people in the stores or sit on their porches; they sought his advice, which they regarded as sacred.

The religious community was also surprised to learn that many sisters and brothers in the community went to him for spiritual direction. Truly, Joe was a "saint." Those living with him over the years treated him patiently and kindly, but few realized how God used Joe to bring good news to so many people. In his brokenness, God's favor was revealed. How important for Catholic evangelization that we recognize God's special presence with people who are developmentally disabled or with those who have been broken by sickness and trials!

Spiritual poverty is rampant as people search desperately for meaning. The deepest spiritual poverty is sin, which interferes with the God–human relationship. By freely turning away from God through serious sin, a person is cut off from the deepest wellsprings of grace and meaning.

Sins committed years ago often continue to gnaw at people. Some believe their sins are unforgivable. Failing to appreciate Jesus' good news of forgiveness, they live in quiet desperation.

Once a female hospital chaplain told me that she sat daily with an old man who wasn't affiliated with any church. Near death, he lingered on. One afternoon, he shared with her an offense he committed years ago. He cried. The chaplain said she believed God forgave him. He answered, "Do you really believe God forgave me?"

"Yes," the chaplain replied. Great peace came over him, as they prayed for God's forgiveness. He died a few hours after she left.

Because of the world's sinful condition and life's imperfections, we may experience other kinds of spiritual poverty as well. One is spiritual meaninglessness, indicated by hollowness in life. In a world where money, power, and sex take precedence over justice, peace, and love, our deepest needs for affection, security, happiness, and meaning often go unattended.

The spiritual yearning for love, understanding, relaxation, and play will not go away. Life is out of hand when play or visiting a friend becomes a chore in an appointment book, carried out on a schedule. The ultimate cannot be programmed. No wonder the Old Testament Scripture says, "Remember the Sabbath day and keep it holy" (Exodus 20:8). The first creation account tells us, "So God blessed the seventh day and hallowed it, because on it God rested from all the work that he had done in creation" (Genesis 2:3). These passages remind us to take time for God, ourselves, and others. Genesis gives us a clue on how to put life in better balance. Keep Sunday holy, praise God, pray, enjoy family and friends, relax, and have fun.

I learned about life's priorities from Sam, a student I had in a college course.

After the first day of class, Sam, a handsome, strong-looking student, approached me. "Father, I'll have to miss one class every other week. Is that okay?" I replied, "Not really, unless you have a good reason." Sam explained that he had a rare blood disease and came close to death two years before.

"Every other week they bring me to the hospital and replace my blood, so I can live for two more weeks." I was stunned as I looked at this man with the physique of a football player. I said, "Sam, you'd better miss class every other week."

As the class progressed, Sam's maturity impressed the students. He never mentioned his ailment. A month before the end of the semester, he wrote a reflection paper. After reading it, I asked him to share it with the class. The day he did, Sam began by rolling up his long-sleeved shirt that always covered his arms. Then he bent his arms and said, "Look at my arms! They are like leather." As he pounded them, they resembled the sleeves of a leather jacket. "They are like this," he continued, "because hospital personnel have stuck hundreds of needles into them to give me blood. Now my arms will take no more needles, and they must find other places in my body to put the needles." Shocked by the appearance of Sam's arms and by his initial comments, the students listened in rapt attention to his story. At one point, he picked up the reflection paper he wrote for me and read:

> What does life mean to you? Is life something you put on every morning like your clothes and walk out the door not giving it another thought? Or is life something you put on like your clothes and walk out the door making the most of every second, of every hour, of every day?
>
> The date is September 12, 1980. The location is a hospital in St. Louis, Missouri.
>
> As I walk down the hospital corridor, I see a young girl smile at me. We start talking and I tell her about my illness and she says she has a tumor at the edge of her brain. Tomorrow, she will have surgery. Sally is only twelve and knows she will be okay, have a malignancy, or come out of surgery paralyzed. It seems so unreal, for she is so young. I almost wish Jesus was there and I could beat on his chest and ask, "Why?"
>
> Sally didn't expect to see me the next morning. They wheel her around the corner where I stand and stop the cart. Sally puts out her arms, we hug, and she looks at me as if to say, "I'm ready." Then they wheel her into the elevator.

When I turn from the elevator, I see the radiator. I kick it so hard that if it weren't attached to the wall, I would have kicked it right out the window. When I kick the radiator, I look up at the ceiling and shout, "Why? She's only twelve! And why did I nearly die several years ago? One day I played in an all-star football game; two days later I woke up sick, and ten days later I discovered I had a rare blood ailment."

Sally is fine today, and I continue to amaze the doctors. Through my experiences I learned something about the "why" of suffering. Even more, I learned to appreciate life. My message is simple: "Make the most of life! Live it to the fullest." For there are people of all ages who would give anything just to walk up the street, just to live a near-normal life.

I know the meaning of suffering, for I have almost died four times. Through suffering, I yearn for life. Nothing means more to me than to wake up to see the light and the smog, for I have learned to appreciate just being alive.

Sam had a tremendous influence on the students. He lived a hopeful message. I never saw him after the semester ended, but his words remain with me, especially his final remarks on that class day: "Miracles do happen! They aren't caused by you or me, but by God. So trust God, no matter what might happen." Faith like Sam's gives root to spiritual meaning, which is the foundation of human activities.

The message of Sam's story is that no effective evangelization happens unless it is rooted in the spiritual. If dioceses, parishes, and individuals live the spiritual message of the gospels, Christians will be inspired to counter today's secular message with a God-centered message that offers ultimate meaning in a functional world. The kingdom of God happens when people turn away from the alienation caused by functional gods to discover healing, health, and wholeness in God's love and human compassion.

Healing, Reconciliation, and Forgiveness

We cannot expect neighbors or work associates to become Church members, when love and forgiveness are not evident in our parishes, organizations, or schools. Today, many people enter the Church through the *Rite of Christian Initiation of Adults*. While involved in this process, catechumens usually experience charity in the small Christian community that develops. But what happens after reception into the Church? Many become disillusioned when they fail to experience a similar response in the larger parish community.

Evangelization demands a reconciling community. We hear about our responsibility to forgive, over and over again, as we assemble for the Sunday liturgy and pray together the most powerful Christian prayer, the Our Father (Matthew 6:9–15) (CCC, #2776).

Since the kingdom of God is gauged by forgiveness, God invites us to re-create the world and society. For Christians, this means the constant call to reconciliation. At times, people find it difficult to see Jesus' example of reconciliation and forgiveness in our parish communities. Parishioners often become disillusioned at the lack of charity in Church leaders who are supposed to symbolize Jesus' message.

Frequently, people working for the Church become disillusioned by politics, infighting, and turf building. While they operate under the banner of Christ, the results of the presence of God—healing, reconciliation, and forgiveness—may not be evident.

Once, I moderated a parish council meeting in a parish that was split into two rival factions. We met on Sunday in a retreat setting. After fifteen minutes, intense group hostility made it impossible to discuss any significant issues. I interrupted the meeting and said, "Stop! Look at what's happening. Since I am coordinating this meeting, I recommend two options. Option one is to go home and enjoy the beautiful afternoon; there is no need to continue this way. The second option is to spend some time alone for two hours, ask God to enlighten us, pray for forgiveness, and then reassemble.

I don't know if we should celebrate Eucharist. If we can't forgive, what meaning will the Mass have, for is it not a remembrance of the kingdom in our midst?"

I asked which option they preferred. They refused to admit defeat and did not want to go home. So we went off for several hours. At five o'clock, the group gathered in the chapel and discussed attitudes and actions. They wanted to celebrate Mass, eat dinner, and meet that evening. I felt God's presence within the group moving them to reconciliation. With their outlook changed, we reassembled and were able to address the business at hand.

Evangelization focuses on the kingdom, which goes beyond Church membership or boundaries. An evangelist is a reconciling person, reaching out to the poor, whatever their religion, nationality, or economic condition, and inviting them to experience God's love. Catholic evangelization is creation-centered, reaching out to people and helping them be reconciled to themselves, others, and God. If evangelization becomes too ecclesial or Church-centered, it misses Jesus' focus on the kingdom and his desire to reconcile all creation to God. It runs the risk of developing into a narrow, one-sided proselytization. Catholic evangelists invite others to become Church members, not to swell parish ranks, but because they believe the Church community is the best way for us to become Christ-like and thus more fully human.

Discipleship and the Kingdom

The *General Directory for Catechesis* says:

> Two thousand years ago he (Jesus) proclaimed the Gospel
> in Palestine and sent the disciples to sow the Gospel in the
> world. Today, Jesus Christ, present in the Church through
> the Spirit, continues to scatter the word of the Father ever
> more widely in the field of the world (GDC, #15).

Today's disciples continue to scatter God's word to the ends of
the earth. This often happens through a mother's love, a father's
sacrifice, a friend's compassion, or a minister's dedicated service. It
happens, also, through a computer specialist's dedicated efforts to
bring modern techniques to Third World countries, a business person's just dealings with employees, a corporate executive's work to
provide food for starving countries, a volunteer missionary's ministry in a devastated area, and the multiple efforts of people to
reach out to the needy. In so doing, the modern disciple continues
to share Jesus' good news in the midst of sadness, fear, and anxiety.
He or she carries out the Lord's calling by sharing hope, freedom,
and healing with those he or she meets.

Disciples of any age continue Jesus' mission of proclaiming the
kingdom of God, a kingdom that promises peace, salvation, and
eternal life. Unlike earthly promises, the disciples share God's
word, knowing that the Lord of heaven and earth is always faithful.
The Christian God is a God that cannot go back on the word of life,
promised by Jesus and sealed by his death and resurrection.

The good news that evangelization proclaims includes a firm
belief that every Christian is called to discipleship. This invitation
is rooted in Baptism and is clarified through a life-long conversion process. In accepting this call to discipleship, the follower of
Christ is confident that he or she will be guided by the Holy
Spirit. As the *Catechism of the Catholic Church* states, ". . . the Spirit
will now be with and in the disciples, to teach them and guide
them 'into all the truth' [Cf. *Gen* 1:2; Nicene Creed (DS 150);

Jn 14:17, 26; 16:13] (CCC, #243). For this to happen, the disciple follows the master by taking up one's cross and following him (Matthew 16:24).

For the faithful Christian, the call to discipleship presents great challenges today, for this calling is lived out in a society whose values often are opposed to those of Jesus. The contrast in values provides a fruitful way to highlight the remarkable depth of Jesus' message. While the relativism, individualism, and secularism of today's world leave many people feeling shallow, lonely, and lost, Jesus' message promises fulfillment and peace that the world cannot offer. The way of Christ is an alternative approach to the tired, worn out promises of a society, which lives as if only today's pleasures count. The way of the Lord, proclaimed 2000 years ago is the ever fresh, new way that the Christian disciple is privileged to announce to the world. Indeed, Jesus' way is good news.

A disciple of Jesus takes up his or her cross. This means a constant desire to grow in faith, hope, and charity. It requires an ongoing effort at conversion to a lifestyle that is generous, patient, and kind. It means the willingness to sacrifice for the truth, speak out against injustice, and use the particular gifts God has bestowed on him or her to build God's kingdom on earth. The disciple is a person of prayer and one loyal to the teaching of Christ and the Church, knowing who he or she is as a Christian, and open to sharing Jesus' message with others. The disciple strives to work with people of other Christian denominations and religious traditions to spread the messages of forgiveness and compassion.

The choice to become a disciple can result from the good example shown in our family, which is God's crucible for fostering faithful discipleship in any age. These beginnings are reinforced by the witness of Christians in the world and celebrated in worship. In many and varied ways, Christian discipleship, rooted in evangelization and the kingdom of God, continues the salvific work of Jesus.

Evangelization, Kingdom, and Discipleship

Personal and Pastoral Reflections

Many Catholics fail to appreciate the richness and scope of the kingdom of God. It is an expression they have heard, but do not appreciate. For one thing, they do not live in a kingdom, so the nuances it presents are missed in our culture. In addition, its past usage often equated it with heaven. For such people, it is difficult to appreciate its reference to life here on earth.

To further an understanding of the kingdom of God among Catholics and to appreciate its connection with evangelization, it helps to reflect on key notions developed in this chapter. Hopefully, this will assist us to further acknowledge our role as disciples of Jesus Christ.

The following guideposts are offered to facilitate such reflections.

1. **Clarifying the meaning of the kingdom of God, as presently used in the Church**
   a. How would you explain the meaning of the kingdom of God?
   b. What points or stories in this chapter helped clarify for you the meaning of the kingdom of God?
   c. What is the relationship between the kingdom of God and the Church? How are they similar? How are they different?

2. **Implications of seeing the relationship between evangelization and the kingdom of God**
   a. What consequences do Jesus' teachings on the kingdom of God have for Christian discipleship?
   b. What does it mean to be a Christian disciple in one's everyday work and associations with neighbors and business associates?
   c. What insights for family living are gleaned from Jesus' teaching on the kingdom of God?
   d. If you were really convinced that you are a disciple of Christ, would you live your life differently? How or why?

3. **Action Steps**
   a. Choose one specific way to apply conclusions derived from this chapter to family, work, and personal life.
   b. Create an opportunity to discuss a story or certain point in this chapter with a parish group, family member, or friend. What practical consequences do you hope will come from this discussion?
   c. Encourage pastoral leadership in your parish to clarify the meaning of the kingdom of God for parishioners during Sunday homilies and to look at the consequences of seeing the parish as a means to share the message of the kingdom of God with the wider community.

EVANGELIZATION, CREATION, AND LIFE

For the people of early civilizations, understanding life without linking it to creation was impossible. They returned to their creation stories to address life's meaning. Basic beliefs were revealed as the community learned the relationship between gods, spirits, people, and nature. These stories acknowledged human limitations, suffering, and death, and pointed to human dependency on powers greater than earthly ones.

In the twentieth century we have become increasingly divorced from nature and creation. A child living in a New York's concrete jungle may be awestruck by the large trees in Central Park. A suburban child who knows nothing but artificial light may never experience the mystery and terror of darkness. And yet, the same energies that pulsated through early cave dwellers move us today.

To appreciate the way Catholic evangelization, rooted in the kingdom, reveals Jesus' good news, we need to understand that creation and life itself are at the heart of God's communication with us. This chapter stresses that God's creative activity continues in partnership with nature and with human endeavors. Several personal testimonies illustrate this reality.

For the Lakota Native Americans, a "vision quest" involves a ritual in which a dream or vision gives direction to an individual's life. The Lakotas believe that an individual discovers the heart of God's self-revelation in one's own story. Before speaking to the tribe, a Lakota leader often shares a personal vision quest. This sharing creates a climate of trust, freedom, and understanding. Sharing spiritual experiences reveals the path that brought the person to God and influenced that person's direction for life.

Perhaps every person has a special moment when God's communication gives the person a hint as to why he or she exists. Mine happened when I was fifteen.

Every day, I walked home from high school, usually with three or four friends. This day, I was alone. I came down to the bottom of St. Lawrence Avenue and began to walk up the other side of the hill. The sun glistened in the bright spring afternoon. Crisp air, new tree buds, and a pesky squirrel surrounded me. Having walked about fifty feet up the hill, I stood under an elm tree with a thick bush on the right. Suddenly, a powerful presence surrounded me. I stopped and looked into the tree. The sparkling sunshine through the new green life seemed to say, "Bob, I have something special for you to do with your life." I felt warm, at peace, and unafraid. I felt whole, together, loved. For a moment, my adolescent insecurities, scruples, and fears ceased. The place where I stood was holy ground. The episode lasted no more than ten seconds, but forty years later I remember it as if it happened yesterday.

While this did not elicit thoughts of a priestly vocation at that moment, I realized in this brief encounter with the divine that life has meaning and purpose. I also saw how we are guided by forces far greater than the chemical or physical laws I studied in school. My adolescent vision quest helped me appreciate that God speaks to us through nature.

Throughout my childhood, my parents encouraged me to love nature. In the woods behind our home, we played, dug small caves, observed animals, and experienced changing seasons. Dad taught me to plant seeds and cultivate tender flowers. Helping him work in the garden, repair broken trees, and cut grass linked me with life's ultimate dimension.

Seminary education halted this process. It almost seemed that I left nature and family behind in the crush of academic studies, rigorous discipline, structured prayer life, and isolation from the world. My early years as a priest continued this pattern. Then, something happened that brought me back to reality.

I taught in the seminary for one year during the late 1960s. A week before my second year was to begin, I was in an automobile accident. Four days later, I lost most of my strength. When this strong, athletic, smart, and confident man did not quickly recover, depression set in. No one knew what was wrong. I cancelled classes and often sat alone in my room for sixteen hours a day, wondering if I would ever recover. Embarrassed, I avoided people, too sick to enjoy their company. Slowly but surely, I was stripped and emptied.

Several years before the accident, I had purchased forty-seven acres of abandoned farmland in Indiana. In deep depression, I walked the land for hours. The trees, especially an old apple tree, became my friends. Often, I sensed God communicating through them. Their broken limbs, yet desire to survive, encouraged me. Gradually my strength returned. I attribute a significant part of my healing to my rediscovery of God in nature, as I walked in the forest, experienced the animals, and sat by my lake.

Then, in 1979, while I was on sabbatical, my father became critically ill. I returned to be with him and Mom the remainder of the year. During Dad's final illness, I journaled on how trees and fragile plant life manifested God's presence to me during my sickness and my Dad's last year on earth.

During the years of my intense sickness, I walked through the woods and admired the strength and struggle of trees. Tulip poplars soared in straight lines above cedars and pines. Oaks stood firm in tornadoes and squalls. Black locusts, brittle and uneven when alive, became like concrete when dried out. I went to the woods whenever I felt tired, nervous, or hurt; often walking for hours, broken and depressed, not knowing where to go or what to do.

I felt the pain of the trees in their struggle to survive. Hardwood trees eventually conquer softwoods in their quest for light. But hardwood trees need cedars and brush to prepare their seedlings. Cedars and brush need grass to cool off the earth. All are in harmony. None give up the struggle until the proper time.

When Dad's sickness came, I stopped going to the woods for a while. When I returned, I had changed, even though the trees remained the same. My old friend, the apple tree, was still there, as were the oaks and walnuts. But I didn't look at them. Instead, I looked to their feet and saw the earth, flowers, and tiny insects that keep the trees alive. I realized that without the smallest, the largest do not live. My perceptions changed from strength to weakness, delicacy, and fragility.

I looked back at the path I created when walking in the grass and observed the cracked plants, broken daisies, and tiny wild roses. I peeked under fallen trees and saw miniature gardens of moss and wild flowers. I stood transfixed every time I discovered a wild flower, which became my new symbol of life in the woods. It didn't matter if I knew the names of my small friends. What, after all, is a moss or flower's name? It is only an artificial label signifying a deeper reality. And the deeper reality is what really counts—a reality expressing beauty, mystery, peace, order, and hope. The deeper reality tells us about an unspoken presence in a gentle breeze, a ray of light, and a touch of beauty—a presence forever constant, yet always elusive.

As I walked through the woods, now looking down at small, fragile life rather than up toward my ancient friends the trees. I said, "Pardon me, my big friends, for neglecting you for a while. My experience with my father causes me to look at those moments of life where waiting, not competition; fragility, not strength; smallness, not bigness, rule. Thank you for sustaining me in the past. Now I look below you at the simple life-giving realities that made you, me, and Dad possible."

Flowers became my life symbols. I meditated upon them for hours, seeing there the deepest life reality. I felt God's immense love sustaining the wild daisy or rose. The delicacy of a thousand flowers, with names unknown to me, pointed to countless nameless and faceless people, that I often pass by without appreciating their beauty or goodness. As I perceived the need to admit my limits and allow my inner self to blossom, I saw life in a new way.

I felt like a flower must feel, almost totally dependent on external circumstances. Life became a matter of survival. Who really knows the deepest rhythms that keep us going? As I reflected on Dad and Mom, on trees and flowers, I discovered the God at the heart of life who teaches us how few are our days. From God and from God's loved ones, we gain wisdom of heart.

As I remember this experience of God's communication through nature, I find it easier to understand how children, adolescents, university students, and adults discover God in a sunset, through a walk in the woods, through pet animals, birds, and butterflies, through family life and friendship.

Some people who experience God in nature find it difficult to participate in organized religious activities. Their communion with God challenges the institutional Church to ask how well ecclesial ministry identifies itself with people's real needs and with the living God of peace, love, and mercy.

How do these personal testimonies relate to evangelization? Looking back on my early life, sickness, Dad's death, and other events, I realize that life itself roots the evangelization process. This grounding is brought to culmination in the revelation of God in Jesus. After describing creation as the foundation of God's designs for human salvation, the *Catechism of the Catholic Church* says, "Conversely, the mystery of Christ casts conclusive light on the mystery of creation and reveals the end for which 'in the beginning God created the heavens and the earth': from the beginning, God envisaged the glory of the new creation in Christ" [*Genesis* 1:1, cf. *Romans* 8:18–23] (CCC #280).

Grounding evangelization in ecclesial policies, programs, or church community without acknowledging that its basic dynamism comes from nature, family, work, and society, as illuminated by the Paschal mystery, dooms it to a shallow and futile existence. Catholic evangelization, then, needs to be integrated with the manifestation of God's creative activity in every aspect of life.

Communication Circles

God communicates with us in different ways. This begins in creation, is reflected in various world religions, intensifies in God's revelation to the Hebrew people, and is climaxed in the Word-Made-Flesh. God's special revelation in the Judeo-Christian tradition continues through the Church. This book distinguishes between revelation and the many other ways that God is manifested to humans.

Revelation refers to generally accepted sources of revelation in the Catholic community (Scripture and tradition), which sometimes are called *special* revelation. They illustrate the ways God communicates personally to humans (GDC, #36). Such communication, fully revealed in Jesus Christ, is realized by the power of the Holy Spirit (GDC, #37).

When referring to the many other ways God is disclosed to humans (for example, through nature, or people) this book uses terms like, manifestation or communication, not revelation. Some people refer to these ways as *general* revelation. A child's smile, a parent's touch, a sunset, a pet dog's companionship, a symphony's harmony, a computer's complexity, a friend's support, a Hindu guru's wisdom, the Koran, the Genesis creation account, the Sermon on the Mount, a theologian's research, or a bishop's pastoral letter communicate the transcendent mystery of God in different yet complementary ways.

While we arrive at deep insights into the God-world relationship through God's various manifestations, we remember that barriers to this communication exist because of God's transcendent otherness and because of our human limitations.

God's communication is filtered through imperfect, foggy prisms, which never allow God's message to be fully understood or appreciated. The *Catechism of the Catholic Church* says "our knowledge is often obscured and disfigured by error" (CCC, #286). No clear, exact answers exist to problems such as evil, suffering, and death, or the mysteries of the world's origins, human destiny, and eternal life. From nature, the best answers we have are still only a hint or suggestion.

We learn beauty from a flower, but beauty transcends flowers. We also experience it in people, in mountains, and in sunsets. Ultimately, beauty hints at beauty's source, a God who makes possible all earthly beauty. In a similar way, we learn goodness from our parents, friends, and colleagues. Long hours of waiting, supporting, and encouraging a sick child or adult reveal the goodness that lies deep within and connects us with God as life's source.

During my sickness that ranged over almost ten years, I often wondered why a good God permitted suffering, depression, and near despair. When personal darkness set in, I learned from the blackness and despair of Jesus' cross that God's energy calls people to life, not death. The cross became my symbol of hope. If Jesus suffered and died, so must I; if Jesus arose, so would I. I learned the paradox of a creature, groping toward wholeness, buoyed up by God's supportive energy.

These insights are examples of how God's communication happens in our lives. They are hints, suggestions, and intimations of God's presence in the world. They're not clear-cut absolute certainties, but lead us closer to God. As the *Catechism of the Catholic Church* says, " In the creation of the world and man, God gave the first and universal witness to his almighty love and his wisdom, the first proclamation of the 'plan of his loving goodness,' which finds its goal in the new creation in Christ" (CCC, #315).

The following model clarifies the way God's communication occurs. This model presupposes that God is at the heart of creation, sustaining it and communicating with it in an ongoing way. Although beyond creation, God is with it, constantly urging us to move from incompleteness and brokenness to wholeness and freedom.

God, at the center of the circles, permeates all levels and exists beyond them. As the circles become larger, they are rooted in the smaller circles from which they take their energies. Let us first examine the upper half of the model: nature, human societies, individuals, and special revelation.

Nature—stars, planets, plants, birds, and humans—mirrors God's presence and grounds all revelation. The arrow flowing

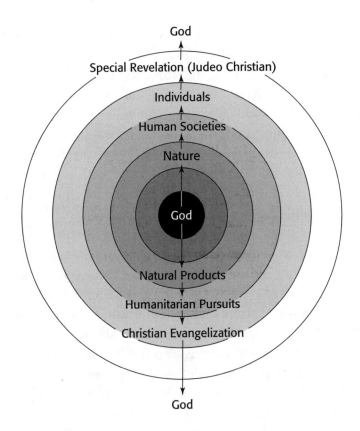

God

Special Revelation (Judeo Christian)

Individuals

Human Societies

Nature

God

Natural Products

Humanitarian Pursuits

Christian Evangelization

God

from God through nature indicates the creative activity between the Creator as the ultimate life source and created nature as the means to communicate God's ongoing creative energies.

Genesis tells us that "God created humankind in his image" (1:27). The human ability to communicate symbolically, to use rational thought processes, to develop scientific and technological theories, and to appreciate holiness, beauty, truth, goodness, and love sets us apart from the rest of creation. These capabilities enable the development of human societies. We have some independence from the rest of the created universe, but when human societies distance themselves too far from the nature from which they evolved and upon which they depend, the rest of the created universe becomes an inadequate and distorted link in the communication with God.

Human societies form the basis for our individual lives. Our families, friends, and ethnic cultures shape our basic human values, such as love, patience, and trust, as well as our conscience, temperament, confidence, and coping abilities.

God first comes to us through people. A parent's love and sacred Scripture disclose God in different ways, but both participate in God's ongoing creative activity. The diagram indicates the role humans play in God's communication with the world by the arrows that flow from God, through nature and human societies, to focus on individuals.

The outer circle indicates that God, in various times and places, has been revealed to the Hebrew people and through Jesus. These revelations further illuminate the presence of God in human experience. Christianity teaches that God's special revelation in the Old and New Testaments and the Christian tradition goes beyond what people can comprehend by natural means alone.

Catholic evangelization needs to ground its activity in God's presence in nature, human societies, individuals, and in the Judeo-Christian revelation. It must remain open to deeper insights into the Christian message that come through dialogue with other world religions, especially their scriptures and traditions.

The lower half of the model represents the activities resulting from dialogue or interaction between the circles. The first is natural products. These result from our using natural elements to produce something. Examples range from a clay pot to a computer. The second category is humanitarian pursuits, where individuals work to better society. Examples include volunteer work in a child-care center, helping a sick person, and assisting tornado victims. The third activity is Christian evangelization. This results from proclaiming God's good news as revealed in the New Testament in light of society's needs or an individual's concerns. Examples include teaching children about God, celebrating Jesus' good news in liturgy, and inviting Christians or non-Christians to listen to Jesus' kingdom message within the Catholic tradition.

In light of God's universal presence in the world, the *General Directory for Catechesis* says "The Christian knows that every human event—indeed all reality—is marked by the creative activity of God which communicates goodness to all beings; the power of sin which limits and numbs man; and the dynamism which bursts forth from the Resurrection of Christ, the seed renewing believers is the hope of Christian 'fulfillment'" [GS, #2] (GDC, #16).

All three categories are important for evangelization. Since God is present in nature and human societies, God is manifested within these two areas independently of Scripture or Church teaching. We need to look for signs of God in our everyday world. A computer, television set, or microscope can open up new avenues for exploring God's presence in our life. They can become eyes to the world, assisting the senses, reason, imagination, emotions, and will to know God and life's meaning more deeply. Humanitarian activities, performed by people made in God's image, likewise manifest God, whether or not they are performed by people who explicitly believe in God.

When I was a child and teenager, working in my father's store, poor neighborhood people taught me concern for the elderly and those less fortunate than myself. Many of these people never went to church, but I sensed God's presence in the way they looked out for an elderly woman living on the third floor of a tenement house and for a person with disabilities who found it difficult getting to the store.

These kind actions, manifesting God implicitly, are similar to Jesus' activities in reaching out to those who were sick and infirm. Christian evangelization, which seeks to relate Jesus' message to our lives, is usually most effective when it integrates its approach with the way God is already implicitly present.

Discovering Meaning Through God's Communication

God can comes to us through nature, human society, special revelation, or products of human ingenuity. This never happens in isolation, for each manifests God in different, yet complementary ways. The following diagram illustrates this reality:

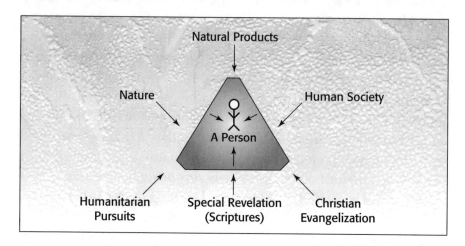

The person at the center of the triangle is molded by God's creative urges named along the longest sides of the triangle—nature, human society, and special revelation. The blunted edges of the triangle—natural products, humanitarian pursuits, and Christian evangelization—result from the intersection of nature, human society, and special revelation.

We are born through the creative energies of God present in the procreative activities of a man and a woman. We filter our experiences through the story of our life. This story includes our genes, culture, consciousness, history, and activities. We are supported and energized by forces rooted in God and filtered through nature, human society, and Scripture.

Constantly formed through this integration, we reach out to discover meaning in the world that shapes us. This lifelong process begins with our parents and continues through family, friends, and society. We are radically influenced by the divine energy or lack of it that comes through experience. Pope John Paul II affirms the importance of experience when he says, "People today put more trust in witnesses than in teachers (EN, #41), in experience than in teaching, and in life and action than in theories" (*On the Permanent Validity of the Church's Missionary Mandate* (RM), #42).

From the beginning of human history, people reached out to discover more than their own lives could provide in their search for God and meaning. Within this context, a society's myths, traditions, and scriptures played a central role. Early cave wall paintings, scraps of parchment, ancient religious writings, statues, and other artifacts indicate that people from the beginning looked beyond immediate experience of this world for ultimate answers to life's meaning, purpose, and destiny. Oral traditions, still evident in Africa, South Seas Islands, and among certain Native American tribes, confirm these written records. Both oral and written accounts describe how God(s) communicated with people at creation's beginning, giving our ancestors direction and wisdom. The myths of origin disclose a tribe's approach to life by manifesting basic earth secrets.

Holy writings often form the sacred center of a community's beliefs and influence people's actions. The Old and New Testaments, accepted as God's special revelation, have a unique role in manifesting the good news of God's love and salvation. The two Genesis accounts of creation set the stage for the Judeo-Christian image of God and salvation.

The seven-day creation account (Genesis 1:1–2:4) emphasizes:

- There is one God.
- God created everything.
- Humans are created in God's image.
- The world is good.
- The Sabbath is holy.

The Sabbath, God's day, is holy, because Yahweh-God is holy. Holiness is God's nature and deepest being. This holiness calls us to holiness. Made in God's image, we are the only earthly creatures that uniquely share God's holiness, can appreciate it, and can bring it into the world. This offers Christians and Jews the primary task of building a world made in the image of the all-holy God.

The first Genesis story describes humans as stewards of the earth, called to act responsibly in mirroring God's creative activity. The Sabbath rest, a day set aside each week for bonding with God and for personal renewal, symbolizes life's transcendent quality and invites us to look more deeply into our lives. Evangelization, based on this biblical insight, regards us as doors to holiness and ministers of peace.

The Adam and Eve account (Genesis 2:5ff) emphasizes:

- Happiness means living in harmony with God (paradise story).
- Sin disrupts that harmony.
- Suffering and death result from sin and the human condition.
- God promises salvation and redemption.

The Adam and Eve story is every person's story. From the beginning, people sinned. With sin came brokenness, pain, and death. We cannot survive alone. We need God, who promises forgiveness and eventual happiness. This account hints at redemption and a future Messiah. Evangelization sees in this account the importance of acknowledging friendship with God as the means to overcome the alienation caused by sin and suffering. Evangelization, while admitting sin's reality, urges us to turn to God and be reconciled.

The themes of these creation accounts reappear in the historical books, the writings of the prophets, the psalms, and other writing in the Old Testament. They also ground Jesus' message, the ultimate source of good news for Christians. The Judeo-Christian story acknowledges:

- God created a world that was good.
- The universe was <u>wounded</u> by sin. (not corrupted)
- Humans have a call to help heal a broken world by sharing God's holiness.
- There is a creative plan, now continuing through human cooperation with God, moving to eventual completion.

This notion of continuing creation sees us as partners with God in creation. It finds new meaning and impetus in Teilhard de Chardin's work. Teilhard de Chardin, a Jesuit priest and scientist, lived during the first half of the twentieth century. His deep spirituality, belief in God's universal presence, and scientific knowledge blended to offer a new synthesis of the God-world relationship. While aspects of his work are controversial, his overall vision of God's creative activity added new insights to the relationship between God and the world.

The holistic view of creation, influenced by Teilhard's vision, includes the following elements:

- Creation is a dynamic, ongoing process.
- The universe, an unfolding reality energized by God, shares in God's ongoing creative activity.
- Humans are the special agents of creation. The future of the evolutionary process is in their hands. Sin can disrupt or destroy this process.
- Creation moves toward redemption in Jesus and toward a final fulfillment in what Teilhard calls the Omega Point.
- The church focuses the universe's love energy, revealed fully by Jesus, into a symphony of service and celebration.

Teilhard's vision implies that God created the world according to whatever science eventually may show is the way the world was formed. God is within, yet beyond, the evolutionary process, which is itself always moved by God's energizing love.

Consequences for Catholic Evangelization

The universe is a continuum; one part influences another through a continuous flow of creative energy. Teilhard's views relate to insights gleaned from Scripture and offer consequences for Catholic evangelization.

1. *Evangelization takes into account our deep life energies.* These primordial needs for nurturing, affirmation, developing self-worth, and understanding one's emotions influence our thought and action. Often the movement of these life energies becomes broken or blocked. Evangelization needs to tie into these wounds in our lives, supporting and reinforcing positive life energies with Jesus' message and the church's ministry. A story from my childhood illustrates this point.

   I sat with Dad and Mom on our front porch during a rain and windstorm. A small tree by the street was split down the center and nearly broken apart. After the storm, Dad and I examined it. I said, "Dad, let's help it get better." He smiled, and we got some tape, rags, string, and nails. He held the tree, and I nailed it together. Then we put tar in the broken places and bound it with rags and string. Some neighborhood kids walked past, laughed, and said, "Cut it down; it will die." I watched the tree every day. In a month or so, it perked up and became strong again. It continued to survive for the remaining twenty years we lived in the house.

   Dad and I helped maintain the basic life energies flowing in the tree. As Catholic evangelizers, we're called to do the same for the people we meet.

2. *Catholic evangelization roots its message in God's holiness, as manifested in our lives.* Holiness influences us more deeply than knowledge. When we encounter individuals who truly live the holiness of the gospel, we are attracted to them. They set the stage to hear the Catholic evangelizer's message. At the same time Catholic

evangelization recognizes the presence of sin and evil as barriers to human fulfillment. This is reflected in the following statement of the *General Directory for Catechesis*, "In light of the Gospel, the Church must appropriate all the positive values of culture and of cultures (cf. EN #20, CT #53) and reject those elements which impede the development of the true potential of persons and people" (GDC, #22).

3. *Catholic evangelization emphasizes the ultimate more than the functional.* The Genesis creation accounts describe human beings as stewards of creation, rooted in living God's holy and loving life. We are called to respond to nature with care and respect, not with domination and abuse. We have a responsibility to build the earth, but too often this leads to functional construction based on an attitude that says, "Science and technology provide the answers to our basic human dilemmas such as war, poverty, and sickness". While science and technology are part of building the earth, Genesis' primary message stresses the ultimate level of love, compassion, and service as the most fundamental relationship between us and the rest of creation.

In organized religion, an emphasis on the ultimate rather than the functional means that prayer, spirituality, compassion, and love are more important than the latest computer, evangelization program, organizational structure, or meeting. While a functional aspect is necessary in any structure, it never touches the deepest energies rooting us to community and God.

Unfortunately, many post-Vatican II parishes, schools, dioceses, and ministers have uncritically accepted a predominantly functional approach. For all the efficiency and good order that follows, the ultimate sometimes gets lost in the shuffle. Our joys and struggles, where ultimate meaning is located, are not orderly or efficient but messy and tentative. The poor, sick, and outcasts, focal points of our ministry, break the models canonized by secular society and some Church organizations. Catholic evangelization needs to opt for holiness and compassion over a coldly efficient organization.

4. *Catholic evangelization acknowledges creation as the ground of God's communication.* Evangelizers assume a humble posture, aware that God comes to us through our families, friends, and society, as well as through other Christian denominations and world religions. This awareness further demands a dialogue that acknowledges other religions as partners in clarifying God's message and giving life meaning.

Catholic evangelization sees all life as divine disclosure. God's revelation in the history of the Jewish people, and in the life of Jesus, point to a unique "God with us" relationship. Catholic evangelization recognizes this immanent yet transcendent God in the fiber of life.

Our experiences disclose God. Just as Moses experienced God on the mountain, we discover God when we walk through the woods or when we climb a steep hill and, from its top, watch a river flow to the sea. We experience God when we support a family member or pray with a friend. When we stop in church to pray and attend Mass, we experience God as ever present, alive, and mysterious. Our God constantly invites us to new levels of meaning. God's revelation to Moses was different from the way we discover God, but the same God and the same dynamic bring us new appreciation.

5. *Evangelization transmits God's revelation to us.* In referring to Saint Irenaeus of Lyons, the *General Directory for Catechesis* says, "God, in his goodness, uses a 'pedagogy' (reference to Saint Irenaeus) to reveal himself to the human person: he uses human events and words to communicate his plan . . ." (GDC, #38). Then, in referring to the continuous transmission of God's revelation, the Directory continues, "The Church, universal sacrament of salvation, born of the Holy Spirit, transmits revelation through evangelization" (GDC, #45).

These passages indicate the intimate connection between evangelization and the kingdom of God and point to evangelization as an important communication channel for God's ongoing presence among us.

Evangelization, Creation, and Life
Personal and Pastoral Reflections

Seeing all of life as a book inviting us to discover, again and again, the abiding presence of God among us helps put God's special revelation through the Judeo-Christian tradition in a new light. This holistic approach keeps ever fresh the truths revealed in Scripture and in the Christian tradition. It also helps us see the close connection between God's revelation in Judeo-Christianity and the communication of God's designs in the other religions of the world.

Seeing God's revelation in relation to creation and life invites us to acknowledge evangelization as the process whereby this revelation continues to be disclosed to the world. It also helps us acknowledge our role as baptized Christians in furthering God's kingdom.

This chapter invites us to reflect on the presence of God in our lives, as well as to see the connection between evangelization and life. To facilitate such reflections, the following reflections and activities are offered.

1. **Reflecting on your story and considering the ways God has walked with you through good and difficult times**
   a. What special times do you recall when God was disclosed powerfully to you? How did such manifestations of God bring about changes in your life?
   b. In what ways could you track God's special blessings in your life by meditating on your journey with God? If you have not done this before, how could you begin?
   c. What stories in this chapter shed insights on God's presence in your life? What were these insights?

2. **Implications of seeing a clearer relationship between evangelization and life**
   a. How do you see the relationship between evangelization, culture, and life after reading this chapter?
   b. What are the consequences in personal, family, and parish life of giving priority to the ultimate rather than the functional?

c. In what ways and times has God been disclosed to you most powerfully in nature, society, family, and Church?

d. What happens to a person's attitude and activities if he or she acknowledges the existence of both good and evil or sin in society and personal life? How seriously do you take the consequences of sin?

e. How would you act differently if you truly believed that you are an agent of God's ongoing creation and redemption of the world?

3. **Action Steps**

a. Find one specific opportunity to apply the insights gleaned from this chapter to your life, family, and work.

b. Look for an occasion to discuss the implications of seeing God's presence in creation with a friend, neighbor, or a church or family member.

c. Arrange an afternoon of reflection in a park or natural setting where you, alone or with others, may ponder God's presence in all of life.

d. Spend a holy hour in church examining the balance in your life between the ultimate and the functional.

e. Encourage your pastoral leadership to reflect on God's presence in life, especially nature, during Sunday homilies or at other times, emphasizing how often young people find God in nature and not in a church. Discuss how this tendency could be seen as a positive way to get young people involved in parish ministry.

CHAPTER

EVANGELIZATION
AND SPIRITUALITY

In the Gospel according to Mark we read:

"In those days Jesus came from Nazareth of Galilee and was baptized by John in the Jordan. And just as he was coming up out of the water, he saw the heavens torn open and the Spirit descending on him. And a voice came from heaven, 'You are my Son, my Beloved; with you I am well pleased'" (Mark 1:9–11).

A close relationship exists between this passage, the Pentecost experience—when the Spirit descended upon Jesus' disciples

(Acts 2:1–4)—and Christian baptism. The message contained in these events is at the heart of evangelization and Christian spirituality.

In Mark, Jesus is proclaimed as God's Son. This happened at the beginning of Jesus' public ministry. His baptism by John initiated Jesus' evangelizing activity, namely, his proclamation of God's *good news* of salvation. On Pentecost, the Spirit descended upon the disciples, thus beginning the Church's mission to evangelize or proclaim the saving reality of Jesus' dying and rising for the sins of the world. The events of Pentecost are seen as initiating the disciples' evangelizing ministry.

In Christian baptism, the Spirit descends upon the baptized, thus initiating us into the Paschal mystery. This action sets the foundation for our response as Christian disciples. During the rest of our lives, we grow into the meaning of our baptism. Baptism is not a once-for-all-event. Baptism, at whatever age, sets the stage for our public profession of Jesus as Lord. It symbolizes our call to serve as Christian disciples, who proclaim the *good news*, as did Jesus' followers after Pentecost. The same Spirit that descended upon Jesus and the disciples descends upon us at baptism, setting the foundation for our response as disciples who evangelize others about the meaning of God's love.

Through living out our baptism, we proclaim Jesus' message of salvation. Hence, the heart of evangelization and Christian spirituality is our call to discipleship. As we follow this call, we come to see spirituality as a process of seeking God on our journey of Christian discipleship.

This never happens in a vacuum. Our growth as disciples is deeply influenced by family and culture, for God shares divine life through people who influence our *yes* of faith. Spirituality is rooted in shared faith. This chapter considers:

- spirituality and evangelization in relation to the challenges of contemporary culture;
- spirituality as a process;
- the elements of an evangelistic spirituality;
- and the consequences of spirituality and evangelization for parish and family lives.

Challenges of a Contemporary Culture

Christian discipleship, rooted in the kingdom of God, happens in the context of culture. The culture of the United States presents unusual opportunities and challenges for evangelization and spirituality.

The Catholic tradition holds that the world is good, but wounded. The first manifestation of God is described in the first creation account (Genesis 1:1–2:4). Here, the sacred author tells us that God created the world and its inhabitants as good. Early people saw God's creation in this way, but they saw something more. They recognized the presence of evil, brokenness, and failure and wondered *"why"*.

The second creation account (Genesis 2:5ff.), telling the story of Adam and Eve, addresses this issue. It says that, after the Fall, God did not abandon us and hints at the redemption of the human race. Catholic theology teaches that, after the Fall, the world was wounded but not corrupted. We find reflections of God's presence in creation, life, and people. Consequently, Catholic spirituality includes nature as an important manifestation of God's presence.

Our good, yet wounded world needed redemption through the life, death, and resurrection of Jesus, the Son of God. This second manifestation of God in Jesus affords us hope and salvation. Jesus continues to live in the world through his body, the Christian community. This belief is reflected in the words, "Jesus, in the parable of the sower, proclaims the Good News that the Kingdom of God is near, notwithstanding the problems in the soil, the tensions, conflicts, and difficulties of the world" (GDC, #15).

Consequently, Christian spirituality begins on a positive tone. We search for God in nature, human experience, and the Church. The *General Directory for Catechesis* states, "The Christian knows that every human event—indeed all reality—is marked by the creative activity of God which communicates goodness to all beings . . ." (GDC, #16).

The Christian disciple brings a positive, hope-filled message to a world that often has no road map, except that provided by materialism, relativism, and secularism. The latter present significant challenges for Christian spirituality. The same worldly pull that draws us away from God creates a vacuum in our hearts that moves us to search for God. We know instinctively that all values cannot be relative, that material possessions and wealth alone cannot bring happiness, and that the hectic pace of society cannot be the answer. Yet, we continue to drain ourselves through work, superficial activities, and frenzied schedules. The same technology, that issued in the contemporary era and shapes our priorities and values, invites us to take another look. Hence, "In light of the Gospel, the Church must appropriate all the positive values of culture and cultures and reject those elements which impede development of the true potential of persons and peoples" (GDC, #21).

Technology is a great gift. Used properly, it builds the earth and brings peace, justice, and freedom. It offers untold possibilities for good when we root it in ultimate values—love, justice, and truth—and see it as a means to an end, not as an end in itself. It affords wonderful opportunities to build a better world through science, medicine, business, communication, research, and travel.

But these benefits have a flip side. The media is fixated on the superficial, stressing relativism, possessions, money, sex, and power. Seen mythologically, the *anti-hero* becomes a god. These underlying values canonize a quantified, functional worldview that knows no variations and leaves little room for ultimate values.

Cultural values, ritualized in the media, affect family life. Often, our busy life resembles a television set. We turn it on in the morning, go-go-go all day, take an occasional time out for a commercial, eat, shop, love on the run, and turn it off to sleep after the eleven o'clock news.

People who live like this rarely have the time to unwind, enjoy nature, experience intimacy, pray, or keep Sunday as the Lord's day. For them, Sunday exists to catch up on the week's chores, for quantifiable, functional values have priority. With little depth in their lives, existing and maintaining on a day-to-day basis becomes the goal.

Today's families struggle to survive, often with little help from society, Church, and family traditions that once established a solid set of values. Families tread uncharted paths, often influenced by popular culture through television, movies, music, books, and advertising. Amidst many pressures, families often try to share ultimate values, like intimacy and love, but secular pressures compete with their efforts to cultivate these values. It is easy to fall into the trap of functionalism without realizing it. A Catholic school teacher who taught second grade for more than forty years said, "I never taught children before who were so spiritually deprived. Many experience the worst kind of spiritual deprivation. Their parents seldom pray with these children or speak about God. Except for school time, some are in day care from 7:00 a.m. to 6:00 p.m. After this, parents shuffle them to fast-food restaurants and through shopping centers well into the evening. They get so many things to appease them that Christmas and Easter have little value."

Marital stress, especially divorce, can devastate children. A third-grade boy was heard to comment, "My daddy's latest girlfriend likes our hamster more than me." A sixth-grade religion teacher offers this insight, "By sixth grade, many kids build a wall around themselves. They have to be "cool." To show emotion means running the risk of getting hurt." Many children assimilate value systems where success and status are more important than integrity. This is evidenced in the comment of a sixth-grade girl who, after hearing Jesus' story, replied, "Did you say that Jesus was a carpenter? How do you expect us to follow him, if he was a carpenter?"

Children need time spent in a relaxed, loving relationships with their parents. The negative scenarios described above do not imply that there aren't loving families who have successfully struggled to maintain healthy, positive relationships. But today's crisis in family life challenges us to look seriously at our relationships and values.

The Christian community makes a tremendous contribution by challenging society to live by deep and authentic values while drawing on the rich potential of modern technology. Jesus' teachings offer a powerful message for people desperately trying to make sense out of our fast-paced lives.

Maturing Spirituality

Evangelization means *sharing the good news of God's love and forgiveness*. Spirituality is *our relationship with God, others, and the world, inspired by the Spirit, as an ongoing response to our call to evangelize and be evangelized*. Like evangelization, spirituality is a process rooted in creation, filtered through community, and influenced by institutions. Five elements have significance for spirituality and evangelization.

Cultural Institutions

Culture has a powerful influence on spiritual formation. I grew up in a Catholic family and neighborhood, attended Catholic schools, and took an active part in parish functions. During these years, my spirituality meshed with that of my family and my friends in our church and neighborhood. Church rituals, family rituals, and personal prayer were consistent.

After high school, I left family, friends, and a comfortable spirituality to enter a college seminary. It was a new world, where spirituality became a regimentation of formal prayer, with little spontaneity and freedom. One day I asked myself, "Where is the God I felt so close to as a youth?" This example from my life illustrates the influence institutions, such as family and church, have in spiritual formation.

Cultural Sensitivity

Efforts to facilitate spiritual growth in family, school, or parish must be sensitive to our individual spiritual tendencies. This requires flexibility. Where sensitivity to individual or cultural needs is absent, negative results usually follow. For example, Maria, a Hispanic woman, entered a convent but stayed only one year. She found it difficult to integrate her spiritual traditions with the community's white, middle class, European values. In the past, African American men entering our seminaries often had a similar reaction.

God Within Us

Regardless of cultural pressures, we are carried along by a force greater than ourselves. Absolute trust in this *greater force*—God—directing human life is essential for our spiritual growth. Who can say why some are given this or that gift, this or that opportunity? Why do others suffer so much? We cannot adequately answer such questions, but we know from our faith that God is with us. When faced with difficulties, the bottom line is what we learn from such experiences. The circumstances, themselves, we cannot control. The deepest motivating force pulling mature Christians into the future is a belief in God's presence. Faith roots our Christian spirituality. By saying *yes* to the Spirit within, we further God's creative designs.

God Within Others

God works in our hearts, even in situations involving pain and suffering. God is present in dysfunctional families and seemingly lifeless parishes. Reflecting on this aspect of the spiritual journey gives us hope when dealing with struggling people or uninspiring catechesis or when experiencing boring liturgies. God is always present, especially with people who are poor or hurting.

Self-Recognition

Christian spirituality is rooted in our personal gifts and baptismal calling. When we forget our roots and take refuge behind roles or masks, our lives lose focus. To be a loving spouse or mother, Sally must first be Sally, who is also a mother and spouse. Jim, to be true to himself, first must be Jim, who is also a businessman, rather than a businessman who happens to be Jim. Recognizing our talents enables us to see that Christian spirituality calls us to be faithful to the way our personal gifts, rooted in the Spirit, direct us to God's kingdom.

Evangelistic Spirituality

These five elements set the stage for a deeper consideration of evangelization and spirituality. Pre-Vatican II spirituality stressed following God's will by following Church beliefs and practices. Post-Vatican II spirituality focuses on responding to God by giving priority to God's kingdom. Though the approaches of these two types of spirituality differ, they are not mutually exclusive as their ultimate goal of union with God is the same.

Contemporary spirituality is linked with evangelization. This means spirituality:

- focuses on creation and the kingdom;
- needs the Christian community to support this kingdom focus;
- acknowledges God's presence in family, marketplace, and society;
- accepts the responsibility to continue God's creative activity in the world;
- responds to Jesus' call to challenge unjust social and Church structures;
- bases its orientation on baptism and the common priesthood of all Christians;
- recognizes the need for sacred time to pray and reflect;
- develops a bond with the Christian community, especially its liturgical and sacramental life;
- probes God's presence in life through relating God's word in Scripture to human experience;
- places high regard on spiritual reading and Church teaching as solid grounding for individual and communal spirituality.

These dimensions of evangelistic spirituality challenge individuals and parishes to consider how the Christian community helps us search for life's meaning. The heart of this quest involves listening and responding to the Spirit of God, often found in our stories.

This came home to me not long after my ordination. My Mom attended a Mass where I was the presider. Afterward, in discussing my homily, she said, "Bob, tell stories." Her words helped me link the Scriptures more deeply with life. When I began to tell stories, my preaching changed. "Why does everyone listen," I wondered, "when a story is told? Why do they get distracted with more technical explanations?" Soon I realized that a story appeals to the whole person—emotions, spirit, and mind—while explanations or examples appeal primarily to the mind.

Evangelistic spirituality, centered on discovering God through shared faith, connects with our stories. Spiritual companioning, shared faith experiences, and directed and preached retreats invite us to see God's work in life. Parish spirituality is inadequate if it fails to help us sort out the Spirit's role in our work, family, and social lives. Spirituality centered on our stories provides a focal point enabling us to develop a value system from within, rather than having one imposed from without.

I also learned about the importance of story from the Native Americans. For them, *the story* frames life. Creation stories, hero myths, and other tribal stories set the parameters for their existence. These stories explain why things are as they are and make fuller sense than rational analysis alone.

Community and individual stories help us make sense of life. For example, Grandma Harie's faith—the Christian story—tells of her reverence for the Eucharist. Mark's faith—the Christian story—inspires him to work with prisoners. Billy's parents' divorce and struggle with alcoholism—his family story—brings fear, when he wonders whether he should marry. Stories are essential to life, for stories manifest who we are, and why we are as we are.

God is present in our stories. To discover God's presence in the human heart, look to the story. Spirituality based on our story invites us to search for maturity. Becoming spiritually mature is a lifelong process which develops at each person's own rate. A fourteen year-old can be more mature than a forty year-old. Maturity is seen in the context of our story. Respecting our uniqueness means acknowledging the personal and social factors operative in our personal growth.

As we reach out to life, we encounter blocks and obstacles. For example, Sam was physically abused as a child. He became quiet and timid, afraid of more rejection. This surfaced dramatically in adolescence when he refused to go to high school. Therapy traced his fear to his early abuse. Sam needed to overcome this block before he could develop his potential.

In another case, Bill and Mary, married for seventeen years, got a divorce after Bill began dating another woman. Mary, devastated by Bill's extramarital affair, became sullen and depressed. It took five years before she got on with her life.

In both examples, traumatic events blocked a person's journey to spiritual maturity. Other examples include failing an examination, being insulted at a party, or having a fight at home. Such situations need to be faced before one can adequately reach out to others. Some blocks may be handled in a few days, others take years.

To become spiritually mature we must reach out to life. Small babies move their hands and arms. Toddlers explore their surroundings. Adolescents begin a search for meaning in their lives. Adults move into a wide variety of experiences that connect us with our inner selves and with other people. This reaching out is essential if we are to probe life's mysteries and to appreciate God's presence. When we reach out, life always responds positively or negatively. As this occurs, we learn.

When I was a boy, my family supported, affirmed, and loved me. Dad played ball with me, our family went on vacations, and Mom helped me with my homework. Grade school and high school continued this supportive environment. I developed self-confidence and a positive outlook in the ups and downs of growing toward spiritual maturity in childhood and adolescence. During this growth stage, self-reflection helped me understand who I was. This self-reflection was rooted in my acceptance by my family, school-mates, and neighbors. I sorted this out to the degree that a child and adolescent can do so. I handled rejection by a few classmates during these years in the broader context of a loving environment. When I went to college, the positive environment changed. The college's rigor, impersonality, and competition contrasted sharply with my home experiences.

One day, while discussing some matter at an assembly, I was ridiculed by a professor. His shredding sarcasm shattered my confidence and made me insecure about speaking publicly. For twelve years afterwards, I fell into a falsetto tone in public speeches. Finally, four years after ordination, when I moved into a very supportive environment, I returned to my natural speaking ways.

Success, affirmation, disappointment, or failure influences our self-image. This happens on a subconscious level. Self-reflection, or taking the time to ask questions about who we are and how events affect us, helps us grow toward spiritual maturity as we deal with these influences. The ever-present God, assisted by family, friends, and counselors, moves us to new levels of awareness.

Through self-reflection, we come to clearer personal insights. This recognition is basic for a mature spiritual life. Personal goals ground the way we reach out to life. Self-reflection helps us ascertain which ones are realistic. Everyone has gifts and limits. Until we appreciate the implications of this reality, we will search for impossible dreams or shy away from realistic opportunities.

Personal outreach needs a focus. Gradually, through life's give and take, we set directions for our life. We gravitate toward certain people and avoid others. We pursue particular career objectives and develop life patterns. We form a value system, influenced by the give and take of our experiences. Secular society perpetrates a massive fraud when it tells us that functional values—values which serve expedient or only practical ends—bring deep happiness. Unless we root life in ultimate values, spiritual maturity is not possible.

A spiritually mature person's value system is consistently directive. Ultimate values help us decide when to say *yes* and when to say *no*. Two stories illustrate this point:

Michael accepted a promotion as vice president of a large corporation. Soon management directed him to perform actions not consistent with his values. His high salary tempted him to go along with their orders. His value system, honed and refined through his family, faith, and prayer, told him otherwise. After consultation with his wife and four children, Michael quit his job. Together, they asked for God's help and decided that each family member would work to support the family, rather than compromise Michael's values.

Sally, a college sophomore, attended a party with friends. Many students, including her date, began to smoke marijuana. One man made sexual advances to her. Insulted and under pressure, she left.

Michael's and Sally's decisions reflect a quality of a spiritually mature person, namely, a consistent value system that they refused to compromise.

Elements of an Evangelistic Spirituality

Evangelistic spirituality, resting on creation and the kingdom of God, takes various shapes and directions, depending on the time, culture, environment, group, and individual. This section considers requirements for and characteristics of evangelistic spirituality.

Requirements for Evangelistic Spirituality

We crave direction, certitude, and roots, all of which the Catholic faith offers us. Catholic beliefs and practices, rooted in Jesus' teaching on the kingdom of God, acknowledge personal freedom and invite us to share a way of life. Evangelization centers on this shared faith, which gives direction to our lives. Evangelistic spirituality requires:

- knowing Jesus' teaching on creation and the kingdom;
- appreciating Catholic beliefs and practices;
- making Jesus' way and Church life important aspects of our life and work;
- acknowledging family and work as central places to share faith;
- developing a spirituality that integrates personal life, family, work, society, and Church into a holistic perspective;
- providing Christian witness;
- inviting others, through deeds and words, to follow Jesus in the Catholic faith;
- welcoming interested persons to investigate the Catholic faith;
- acknowledging God's presence in creation, culture, various Christian denominations, the Jewish faith, and world religions;
- allowing Christian values to be unifying factors in our personal and communal life;
- and recognizing the presence of the living Lord at the heart of family and work as the basis for our union with God.

Evangelistic spirituality invites us to reach out to others. This may include sharing faith in a family, struggling for justice in society, or participating in missionary activities. It also acknowledges that spirituality, rooted in faith, influences our actions. A spiritually mature person's life revolves around a faith that challenges society's materialistic orientation and invites us to focus on love, justice, mercy and compassion.

Evangelistic spirituality continually invites us to respond to God's presence. Spirituality may be evident in people with little or no Church affiliation. At times, God's mysterious ways leads some people, with little or no family faith, to deep personal belief and action. Their God-given gifts often encourage them to develop ultimate values and move them toward social awareness or humanitarian concerns. Dialogue with such good people teaches us about Jesus' call to serve those who are poor and needy.

Individually and collectively, we search for ways to know ourselves. Self-help books, support groups, counseling, spiritual direction, and other techniques continue to grow in popularity. Evangelistic spirituality offers us a valuable opportunity in this regard. It says, "Our deepest reflection on life's meaning is based on relationship with God." We believe God is loving, healing, holy, just, powerful, and beyond our comprehension. We also believe that God calls us, created in the divine image, to become holy and to live forever with God.

Evangelistic spirituality enables us to learn more about God by reflecting on our experiences, Jesus' teaching, and the Church's beliefs and practices. These are illustrated in the following stories:

Esther and Bill, both unmarried, lived together. Until they attended a parish renewal session, neither thought much about the implications of their way of life in light of Jesus' teaching, Christian beliefs, and the negative example this lifestyle gave to family members and neighbors. This new realization moved them to live apart until they made a decision about marriage.

Irma, a bookkeeper in a business office, altered the books regularly at the request of her boss. Not until she heard a homily about justice did Irma seriously connect Jesus' teaching on justice with her responsibility to live justly. After that experience, she gradually recognized God's presence in her work as an important element of her emerging spirituality. The self-reflection associated with evangelistic spirituality moved her to find work in a more honest environment.

Characteristics of Evangelistic Spirituality

Christian faith sees Jesus as a fully human and a fully mature individual. This perspective roots the following characteristics of a mature evangelistic spirituality.

- Evangelistic spirituality situates our relationship with God and the world in creation.
- Jesus' spirituality links us with God through Jesus' teaching on the kingdom, found in the New Testament. A kingdom-based spirituality sees healing, forgiveness, and reconciliation as center points linking broken humanity with God. Becoming fully human means loving God, serving others, and working for justice.
- Evangelistic spirituality knows that becoming a holy person is a lifelong quest. The prologue of John's gospel describes the Word (Jesus) as existing from the beginning and disclosing himself in time. This hints at a transcendent quest, inviting us to join with Jesus in a lifelong journey to God.
- A spirituality based on sharing faith is alive with God's Spirit. It motivates us to action by stressing our vocation to share God's life with others. A spirituality based in faith brings life and freedom into our active search for meaning.
- Evangelistic spirituality includes all aspects of our lives, especially family, personal life, work, friends, society, parish, and nature. It treats people of other races and religions as God's children, acknowledges different methods of prayer and spirituality, and allows for diversity. The spiritually mature person acknowledges the whole world as the arena of God's presence.

- Evangelistic spirituality distinguishes good from evil, virtue from sin, and stresses a steady course and coherent value system in our life journey. A consistently directive motivation provides a unifying basis upon which we decide and act, whether in church, at home, with friends, or in the marketplace.
- A spiritually mature person is open to change and growth, eager to investigate life, and to probe deeply the meaning of faith. This person overcomes fear with faith, guilt with love, and learns from various religious and secular sources.
- Spiritual maturity recognizes all people as equal before God. This leads to dialogue where people are respected, not controlled or manipulated. Evangelistic spirituality acknowledges that God's love often comes through human love. A spiritually mature person knows the importance of love, which begins in God.
- Evangelistic spirituality brings new insights, for it discerns our activities in light of God's revelation, Church teaching, and social response. A spiritually mature person acknowledges the Holy Spirit as the ultimate source of our wisdom.
- The spiritually mature person recognizes human limits and sees the wisdom of God becoming human and dying for sinful creatures. This paradox is the basis for Christian faith.
- Evangelistic spirituality acknowledges God's playfulness, patience with weak human beings, and tolerance of failure, as well as God's justice, fairness, and truth. The spiritually mature person, while admitting guilt and fear, is not overcome by them. The humorous and playful characteristic of evangelistic spirituality reminds the spiritually mature person that we are human and God is God.
- Evangelistic spirituality finds its apex in the communal celebration of Jesus' ongoing dying and rising in the Eucharist and other sacraments.

Since God loves us, we must love one another; since God forgives us, we must also forgive ourselves and others. Evangelistic spirituality admits human limits, faults, sins, and the folly of taking ourselves too seriously. It is not complacent or excusing, but it accepts life after death, hope in difficult times, and new opportunities after failures.

Evangelization finds its deepest meaning in our spiritual quest, where God's presence in creation and faith reach fulfillment. Our faith life bears fruit to the degree that we respond to the spiritual yearnings of our heart. Here, God is present and fully alive.

If we experience God's love in the love we have for one another, and share this love in word and deed, evangelistic spirituality takes care of itself. The Christian message is taught, celebrated, and lived, when Jesus' way becomes our way of love, for human love is the deepest manifestation of God's good news.

Evangelization and Spirituality
Personal and Pastoral Reflections

Recently a parishioner said, "Why doesn't the parish do more to support us spiritually? We get little help from society and not much more from the Church. Parishes need to make a commitment to help us grow in faith. Unless they do, parishes will become increasingly irrelevant."

How can parishes address this challenge? Parish evangelization begins by taking into account the many ways that culture influences families, individuals, and the values of today's Catholics. To succeed, evangelization has to be rooted in the family and respond to the pressures of modern society, especially in the marketplace. How this happens will vary from parish to parish.

1. **Reflecting on the relationship between evangelization and spirituality**
   a. To what extent is a family focus central to your parish's activities? How do parish events—RCIA, catechetics, school functions, children's sporting activities, and other parish events—separate or bring family members together?
   b. How is family life affected when a parishioner spends a great deal of time in parish ministry? In what ways does the parish send out subtle messages about values by pulling busy people away from their homes to work excessively for the Church?
   c. How do Sunday homilies support families, single parents, divorced or blended families, and single people and give practical ways to apply Scripture readings to everyday life?
   d. What parish activities show that your parish values as important family and Church members, hurting families, single parents, divorced or blended families, and single people?

e. How do parish ministers and programs teach parishioners, especially children, young adolescents, and young adults, the skills necessary to develop Christian values in a computerized, technological culture?

f. In what ways do your parish liturgical celebrations address the spiritual hungers of parishioners?

g. In what ways does the responsibility for alleviating today's spiritual hunger lie with the parish and how do Christians themselves share in this task?

2. **Implications for Christians in light of an evangelistic spirituality**

a. To what degree do your values center on money and possessions? What are your deepest values? Which of your values may be out of focus?

b. In what ways do you set priorities in your personal, family, and professional life? How are these priorities reflected in your lifestyle and time commitment? What does the amount of quality time that you spend with family members say about your priorities? What can be done to focus your priorities?

c. How are skills for everyday living taught in your family? To what extent do such teachings stress ultimate values—love, forgiveness, justice—or functional ones—money, greed, jealousy, cutting corners?

d. What communication problems do you have with certain family members? How can this improve? What is your level of intimacy with each family member? How can you grow together in love?

e. In what ways, if any, do you control the time your children spend on TV, computer, or video games? How do these things inhibit the communication between family members? How do you help your children develop the skills necessary to sift out acceptable and unacceptable moral messages found in TV programming or on computer sites?

f. How are your Sundays, God's days, set aside for God's honor and your personal renewal? In what ways is Sunday a holy day in your family? In what ways is it not? What more can you do to make Sunday a family day?

g. What are good ways and times for your family to pray together? What kinds of example do you as parents show to children by praying with them and each other? What are the best times for your private prayer?

h. What can your parish do to make sure that Sunday parish activities are limited to Mass and religious instruction?

3. **Action Steps**

a. Identify one specific way to apply insights gleaned from this chapter to your personal life.

b. Discuss with a few friends, neighbors, or parishioners the key areas involved in an evangelistic spirituality.

c. Suggest that your parish offer opportunities for parishioners to explore spirituality as it centers around Scripture and the pressures of today's world.

d. Take an afternoon off and spend it in a natural setting, reflecting on what struck you in this chapter.

e. Attend Mass one extra day each week, asking the Lord for deeper insights into God's presence in the midst of your busy world.

f. Reflect on your responsibility to be a disciple in the workplace.

g. Take concrete steps to pray more in your everyday life.

h. Pray to Mary and Joseph, asking them to intercede with Jesus to grant you wisdom in dealing with issues that arise in your family.

CHAPTER
5

EVANGELIZATION
AND CONVERSION

C atholic evangelization invites us to pattern our lives after
Jesus. We discover the Lord through the lived witness and testimony of other people. Such personal witness is a powerful reflection on the meaning of faith. It helps us see life in a new way and
is at the heart of conversion. The following personal experience
clarifies this aspect of evangelization.

In the spring, I went to a folk festival where booths of arts and crafts extended for two city blocks. In one booth, I spotted a beautiful painting of a thin old man with a wrinkled face and sun-dried hands, dressed in work clothes and holding a wooden mallet, poised and ready to crack a shingle from a block of oak. Something about the old man captivated me.

As I stood gazing at the picture, the boothkeeper said, "It's really something, isn't it? The price is also something—four thousand dollars. A local artist painted it. The shinglecracker lives near here. In fact, you can watch him crack shingles in a booth just over that hill to the right of my booth."

Interested in meeting the shinglecracker, I walked up the next line and found him speaking to a small boy and his father. On one side of his booth were several hundred cracked shingles; behind them stood large oak tree trunks, cut into pieces the length of a wooden roof shingle. At the other end of the booth, the shinglecracker showed the boy how to crack a shingle.

The old man impressed me more than the picture. His worn hands revealed two knuckles missing, possibly from a past accident with the mallet and wedge. He put the wedge on the oak trunk, then struck it with the mallet, and the shingle split.

After the boy and his father left, I spoke with the shinglecracker. He said, "Did you see my picture?" When I said, "Yes," he continued. "Yesterday, after they put it up, I went over and stood in back of the booth. Many people admired it. When I heard their kind words, I tapped one fellow on the shoulder and said, 'The copy is great, but turn around and look at the original. It's better.' It was nice to see their smiles as they looked at me."

I thought about how much they charged for the painting, which wouldn't have been possible without the original to portray. It struck me how often we look at the copy and never get to the original. Soon my thoughts turned to faith. Humans, made in God's image, are beautiful copies of a divine image. Our beauty, however, fades when we fail to mirror the original. It is never enough to stop with the copy, no matter how splendid. To appreciate life we must return to the original and let this image shine.

For Christians, the original is Jesus. In living by his example, we discover life's meaning.

Evangelization demands that we look at Jesus, the original, and pattern our lives after him. In doing so, we become like the original. As St. Paul says, "It is [now] no longer I who live but Christ who lives in me" (Galatians 2:20). This is the heart of life and the basis of Christian spirituality.

This chapter considers evangelization and conversion. It examines various dimensions of God's presence, the meaning of conversion, kinds of conversion, and methods to facilitate conversion.

Dimensions of God's Presence

God seeks us from our birth. Evangelization begins as we experience the beauty of life, parental love, and the marvels of creation. This happens as God's created world touches the core of our being, where God dwells. As we grow, our reflections clarify God's presence. Through such reflections, we discover God's presence in various life dimensions. We describe these as core, community, and consideration dimensions.

God's Spirit dwells at the *core* of who we are. A *community* of loving people nourishes this presence. Here we receive care, support, and affirmation. When we analyze the movement from core through community, we operate in the *consideration* dimension. Our thought processes clarify God's presence in our lives.

We image these three dimensions as aspects of a burning candle. God's divine energy, lighting the wick, represents receiving life and the Spirit's indwelling. The hot, blue inner core of the flame represents our *core* dimension. The oxygen necessary to keep the flame burning signifies the *community* dimension. The purer the oxygen supporting the flame, the more completely it burns. A similar analysis applies to our lives. A loving and supportive human environment helps God's Spirit within us to mature. Just as the candle needs oxygen to keep the lighted candle burning, we need family and loved ones to mirror God's presence. The red, imperfectly burnt parts of the flame at the edges symbolize the *consideration* dimension. This represents the imperfect parts of our lives where we need to analyze our beliefs, study Catholic teachings, and examine life happenings to see how God is present.

Core

The *core* dimension is the same for all people. We have common needs for affirmation and support. We question our identity and ask why we were born, why do we suffer, what is life's meaning, and what happens after death. We have common core needs, because we are human.

Josh sat at the banks of the Ganges River in India. He was the only Westerner there, among countless Hindus. As they meditated and walked into this holy river, he felt deeply connected with the people around him even though he knew none of them by name. A powerful transcendence overcame him as he became one with them. Such a feeling was possible because those assembled were connected at the core, even though their age, religion, and culture differed.

God's presence at our core links us with a similar presence in other humans. Because we connect at a level deeper than race, age, sex, or religion, we identify with others in their needs, aspirations, sorrows, and joys. We connect on this level through other peoples' stories or personal experiences.

Community

God's presence, rooted in the core, is disclosed through creation and *community*. As seen above, community is like the air we breathe or the oxygen needed to sustain the burning candle. Family, friends, and Church focus the energies coming from our core. Hinduism and Judaism filter these energies differently than the Roman Catholic and Baptist denominations.

Christians believe that God' presence, manifested in time and space, is centered in Jesus' dying and rising. The historically different times and social environments where humans live impact the way they formulate beliefs. The core energies of European Catholics are filtered differently than those of North Pole Eskimo Catholics. In conversation with a Catholic Eskimo, I learned first hand how our core beliefs agreed, but how our cultures manifested them differently.

Twenty years ago, I taught an Eskimo woman in a graduate liturgy course at the University of San Francisco. She said little during the entire session. I did not know her background until the course was nearly over.

After I spoke to her, I realized how different were our worlds. She gave me a small book about her native tribe, which I still cherish. After the semester ended, I often wondered how much she got out of the course. I realized that although we both professed the same Catholic beliefs, our traditions differed greatly when it came to celebrating our Eucharistic liturgies, Baptisms, marriage celebrations and other religious rituals.

More recently, I addressed an international conference on "Christian Adult Formation" in Toronto, Canada. In the ensuing years between my San Francisco course and this Toronto conference, I learned much more about Native American customs. After my presentation, a woman thanked me for my stories and comments, which she said, connected with where she was on her spiritual journey.

I suspected that this woman was a Native American. She told me she was an American Eskimo, who lives near the North Pole. She, too, gave me some literature, telling me of her small native village and their Catholic Church. She connected with the core of what I was addressing as a human being and a Catholic, although our worlds were vastly different.

From these two experiences, and many others like them, I learned how Catholics from different cultures, ages, and backgrounds can manifest their beliefs differently, while remaining faithful to core Catholic beliefs.

Consideration

Operating in the *consideration* dimension through rational reflection on core beliefs, the Church formulates dogmas, creeds, theological statements, and pastoral models. Examples include the Church's teachings on the Trinity, Jesus, sacraments, and moral teachings.

The consideration dimension makes it possible for us to shift our theological and pastoral focus in light of changing social circumstances. The models developed enable us to communicate our beliefs to others, pass them on to subsequent generations, write religious books, develop Internet websites, and deal with practical issues. The models coming from such reflections help us plan ways to effectively proclaim God's evangelizing word, examine our motivation, and set new life directions. Although the consideration dimension is compared to the outer red flames at the edge of the burning candle, it is important in theological and pastoral endeavors, including evangelization efforts.

Meaning of Conversion

For many Catholics, the term *conversion* means joining the Catholic Church. This was the common understanding before Vatican II. Today, the term is used broadly to mean growing in and appreciating more fully our relationship with the Lord. This is an ongoing process, as we deepen and refocus our attitudes, energies, life patterns, and loyalties in light of Jesus and Church teachings. Conversion is our lifelong journey to God, on which road we continually say *yes* to God's evangelizing word.

The *General Directory for Catechesis* connects faith and conversion. It says, "Faith involves a change of life, a '*metanoia*,' [Cf. EN, #10; AG, #13b; CCC, #1430–1431] that is a profound transformation of mind and heart; it causes the believer to live that conversion. . . ." [EN, #23] "By meeting Jesus Christ and by adhering to him the human being sees all of his deepest aspirations completely fulfilled" (GDC, #55).

Incentives for conversion come from nature, people, society, and Church. Evangelization is the invitation and conversion is the response. Seen in a holistic way, this movement is called the *evangelization-conversion process*.

Conversion, like evangelization, can be implicit or explicit. *Implicit conversion* means developing positive attitudes toward life or changing one's outlook as a result of a dialogue with life itself with no explicit reference to God.

When I was a small boy, two events affected my general outlook toward life. The first happened when I was in the first grade. I became sick, and the doctor said I had to stay away from school for six months. For many children this would have meant repeating the first grade. But my mother taught me. Every day she spent hour after hour showing me how to spell, read, write, and add. Her goodness, patience, and love gave me confidence. Each afternoon, Mom walked to school, talked to the teacher to get the lessons for the next day, and then taught me. When I returned to school, I was ahead of the rest of the class.

The second event happened three years later. During World War II, a group of neighbors planted victory gardens in the empty lot behind our home. A successful businessman living up the street, who grew up on a farm, befriended me. He taught me to prune tomatoes, grow pole beans, hoe radishes, and prepare the soil for planting.

A poor-sighted old man named Sam had a patch of tomato plants in his garden at the end of the lot, where the soil was rocky. Every day he watered his plants, tried to hoe them, and waited for tomatoes. But the small green ones that appeared on the vines soon withered from lack of nourishment. The old man kept watching for red tomatoes. Since his eyesight was not good, I sometimes tried to help him find red tomatoes on his plants.

One day my businessman friend said, "Bob, we are going to assist nature and make old Sam happy. Only a miracle will put ripe tomatoes on his plants. So we'll make this miracle happen." He took some nice red tomatoes from his garden but left about two inches of green stem on each tomato. Then we went to old Sam's patch and tied the ripe tomatoes on Sam's plants with very thin green thread. When Sam discovered the ripe tomatoes, he called me over and said, "I'm satisfied now because I have ripe tomatoes." My businessman friend professed no religion, but somehow what he did for old Sam stuck with me and disclosed another facet of human responsibility.

As I grew, experiences like these, coming from God's presence in life itself, influenced me. Reactions to such events involve implicit conversion.

Explicit conversion directly refers to God or Jesus in some way. It identifies the God present on our life journey. This awareness often comes gradually. During the months I stayed home from school, Mom taught me about God's love in my sickness and prayed with me. Slowly, the implicit conversion I learned from her goodness became more explicit, when I sensed God's presence healing me. In the same way, years after the victory garden experience of tying tomatoes on Sam's stalks, I learned that God helps people, as we helped Sam. The gardening experience taught me to see God's all-encompassing providence. When I connected these childhood events with God, the early experience of implicit conversion became explicit.

Christian conversion is a gradual process. It has one aim: ". . . a complete and sincere adherence to Christ and his Gospel through faith. Conversion is a gift of God, a work of the Blessed Trinity" (RM, #46). Inspired by the Spirit, which ". . . opens people's hearts . . .", life experiences are constantly reintegrated into a person's personality as one deepens, shifts, or changes life's priorities (RM, #46). Life events have varying degrees of significance, but God is present in the entire process. Hence, Christian conversion means taking on the mind and heart of Jesus as we grow in appreciation of life's meaning. The *General Directory for Catechesis* stresses continuing conversion when it says, "Faith is a gift destined to grow in the hearts of believers [CT, #20a]. Adhering to Jesus Christ, in fact, sets in motion a process of continuing conversion, which lasts for the whole of life" [Cf. RM, #46b] (GDC, #56).

Conversion to the Lord can be seen in two ways. The first sets the foundation for Christian discipleship. It involves deepening our realization of what Jesus' command, *Love God and one another*, means. As conversion intensifies, we see our call to discipleship through the lens of this great commandment. Our attitudes and actions change because we see the implications of living this commandment.

The *second* way conversion helps us appreciate our lives and discover deeper meaning is the recognition of special gifts God gives us. In using these gifts as a laborer, teacher, computer operator, nurse, businessperson, writer, contractor, student, or waiter, we identify our work as a special opportunity to proclaim God's evangelizing word.

Our conversion invites us to see more deeply how God's call to discipleship is especially applicable in family life. In discerning the Lord's call, we pay particular attention to the family aspect of Christian discipleship.

Kinds of Conversion

People come to conversion in different ways—gradually or radically. *Gradual conversion* happens in life's give and take from childhood to old age. Most people come to God in this way and can point to no single event as a definitive moment of conversion. Gradual conversion happens in unperceptible ways, as the Lord gently calls us to discipleship. A paradigm of such an invitation is found in the story of "Samuel" where God calls Samuel four times. Finally, Samuel recognizes the call. Then, as the priest Eli instructed him, Samuel replies, "Speak, for your servant is listening" (1 Samuel 3:1–10, 19). In a similar way, the Lord called Peter, Andrew, and most of his apostles and disciples (John 1, 35–42). The same is often true in our journey to God.

Radical conversion is indicated when a person can point to a definite experience that dramatically altered his or her life direction. Jesus called Paul in this way (Acts 9:1–18). On the road near Damascus, a light surrounded him and the Lord spoke to him. Falling from his horse, Saul conversed with the Lord. This sudden, radical encounter with Jesus changed Paul and he became a new person.

Often, radical and gradual conversions occur together. The gradual process of conversion may be affected by radical events that force a person to change focus. Even with radical conversion, the process is ongoing, as we gradually integrate such experiences into life's overall framework.

Sometimes a traumatic experience challenges one's faith. People often find the Lord through such an event. This happened to Jim. He had no active faith, though he was raised a Catholic. Then his child developed a rare disease that immobilized her. This changed Jim's outlook, and he became a devout believer, who impressed others by the way he cared for his child. His child's sickness deeply changed his faith life.

At other times, difficult experiences lead to loss of faith. This happened in the case of a woman who never attended church again after her child's sudden death. Previously this woman went to Mass regularly.

Many key moments in the conversion process converge around significant rites of passage. Positive ones may include a child's birth, beginning school, First Communion, graduation from elementary and secondary school, and marriage. Negative experiences may include a family member's death, divorce, sickness, job loss, or old age.

The conversion process can be seen in the following illustration. You can probably draw a similar conversion pattern for your own life.

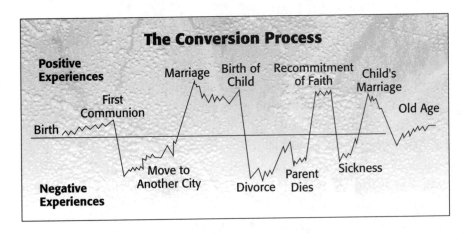

A deeper understanding of life's mystery centered on faith and a greater commitment to love God and neighbor are goals of conversion. As we mature, it becomes clear that full happiness cannot be realized on earth. As Saint Augustine said, *"Our hearts are restless and they cannot rest until they rest in you, O God"* (Confessions, Book 1, Chapter 1). The journey to God has many ups and downs. These peaks and valleys jar us into deeper appreciation of life's ultimate purpose and trigger implicit or explicit conversion.

Since the transcendent God does not operate the way we do, conversion has many faces and cannot be programmed. One experience that changed my spiritual focus happened in the simplest way.

After a retreat, I spent another day in silent recollection. My life was going well. There were pressures, concerns, and irritations, but I was happy and fulfilled. I went to bed late that night. Early the next morning, while waking up, a powerful experience overcame me. Immediately I arose and jotted an expression on a piece of torn paper to remember the experience. Had I not, the event would have been lost. I wrote, "This morning I came to an awareness that I was being touched by a reality so deep that my whole inner self became suffused with meaning". As the *General Directory for Catechesis* says, "Faith and conversion arise from the *heart*, that is, they arise from the depths of the human person, and involve all that he is" (GDC, #55).

The goal of conversion is to fill our inner core with meaning. This comes from God, for God alone gives us meaning. Christians believe our inner core connects with the saving graces won by Jesus. The *General Directory for Catechesis* speaks of this when it says, "The option for faith must be a considered and mature one. Such searching, guided by the Holy Spirit and the proclamation of the *Kerygma*, prepares the way for conversion which is certainly 'initial' [AG, #13b], but brings with it adherence to Christ and the will to walk in his footsteps. This 'fundamental option' is the basis for the whole Christian life of the Lord's disciple [Cf. AG, #13; EN, #10; RM, #46; VS, #66; RCIA, #10] (GDC, #56b).

Methods to Facilitate Conversion

Conversion helps us appreciate life's meaning. This happens *individually*, as we walk our personal faith journey. It also occurs in *community*, as we journey together on our path of faith. Our communal walk with God begins in families and is supported by other Christian believers. On this faith journey, individual and communal conversions connect.

Efforts to facilitate individual conversion center on shared meaning. Our relationship with God roots all shared meaning. Although individual conversion is a personal search, community is central to it. In community, God is disclosed and a person is supported. In stressing *community* in adult faith formation, *Adult Catechesis in the Christian Community* states, "One of the most valid criteria in the process of adult catechesis, but which is often overlooked, is the involvement of the community which welcomes and sustains adults" (ACICC, #28). These words infer that every parish is challenged to maintain a healthy balance between individual and communal conversion in its life and ministry.

Helping others on their faith journey means acknowledging God's presence in creation, family, church, recreation, work, prayer, friendships, and neighborhood activities. Facilitating conversion involves seeing God in life's totality and developing methods to assist people in their response to God.

A difference exists between conversion and methods to facilitate it. Made possible by divine grace, conversion happens between God and a person or a community. Conversion is the goal; methods are means to attain this goal.

Parishes assist this movement to conversion. This happens in catechetical ministry, RCIA, youth ministry, Bible sharing, and adult faith discussion groups. These facilitate the communication between the person and God. Recognizing diverse Catholic populations reinforces the need for flexible methods to facilitate conversion. Such methods, aiming at the core, are fruitful ways to evangelize.

No one best method exists to facilitate conversion. Various methods can be used at different phases of the conversion process.

As the *General Directory for Catechesis* states, "The Church, in transmitting the faith, does not have a particular method nor any single method" (GDC, #148). Effective methods take into account the person, the environment and the facilitator's gifts. At the heart of every method is patience, understanding, love, and trust.

This becomes apparent when we look at the give and take between family members. Here, flexibility is important. In family settings, prayer shifts as children grow. The best environment to bring families closer to God is a loving home.

Family faith grows in ordinary and special life circumstances. Kindness, patience, understanding, forgiveness, and love cement family ties and invite ongoing conversion. Families celebrate birthdays, religious feasts, and special events. Formal methods, like teaching children the Lord's Prayer or having an Advent wreath, deepen the conversion happening through informal family relationships.

Methods are secondary to conversion itself. Saying the family rosary after dinner may be a more useful method in some families than in others. Attendance at Sunday liturgy may be seen differently by various family members. If a teenager refuses to attend Sunday Mass, a parent, after a serious discussion with the teen, might conclude that the young person is not lazy but is struggling with a faith problem. Forcing this youth to attend Mass may do more harm than good. Instead, a parent might help a son or daughter grow in faith by discussing Scripture and applying its message to the teenager's life. Gradually, this may lead to a better appreciation of the Mass.

What works to help one person's faith growth may not be useful for another. Parishes differ and individuals within them are not the same. Hence, the RCIA and catechetical ministries need to employ flexible methods. When flexibility is not maintained, we risk absolutizing a method. If this happens, the method becomes more important than conversion itself.

Since various methods can facilitate conversion, selecting a method depends on the people involved. In one instance, a method centering on prayer, Scripture, or dialogue may be the most effective.

In another, a didactic approach may be better. In speaking of adaptation to different people and circumstances, the *General Directory for Catechesis* states, "Adaptation is realized in accordance with the diverse circumstances in which the word of God is transmitted [Cf. RM, #33] . . . It shall be remembered that, in the plurality of situations, adaptation must always keep in mind the totality of the person and his essential unity, in accordance with the vision of the Church" (GDC, #170).

We come to God differently. Sometimes we need time alone to enhance conversion. At other times, we prefer limited group interaction or more intense dialogue. Such personal preferences influence how we relate to God and others. Because our attitudes affect the conversion process, methods and content materials need to connect with our experience. In so doing, effective methods move beyond community and consideration to the core.

In communal conversion, we distinguish natural groups, like separated and divorced people or children who have lost a parent, from more random groups, like a youth catechetical group or an adult enrichment group. A common concern links natural groups; random groups have no such binding force. Such differences are significant in selecting a method. One method may work best for a given group, leading people to deeper faith, better appreciation of community, and more profound links with God. The bottom line in selecting any method is conversion, not method.

Conversion centers on our search for God in a fractured world, where common brokenness is the starting point. Here, Jesus offers healing and leads us to life's core dimension, where God dwells.

Today's complex world invites us to return to the gospel message of love. Here, we recognize people's diversity and evangelize in light of it. We proclaim the *good news*, as we remember how Jesus taught. He preached a message, often in story form, and challenged his hearers to consider its consequences. We evangelize, as we find new meaning in his Word-made-flesh.

Evangelization and Conversion
Personal and Pastoral Reflections

Conversion is a lifelong process. At various life moments we experience God's presence in nature, home, work, or Church. Gradually we discover the depths of Jesus' good news, brought to fulfillment in his dying and rising. We realize the import of God's love, as we experience the dyings and risings in our lives.

Conversion means seeing in a new way. Often this occurs in the solitude of our heart; at other times, it happens with others. To become more sensitive to conversion moments, reflect on key notions gleaned from this chapter. This can be done alone or with others.

The following guideposts are offered to facilitate such reflection.

1. **Considering the relationship between conversion, individual faith, family life, and work**
   a. What points or stories in this chapter helped you better appreciate the presence of God in your life?
   b. Reflect on moments of conversion in your family. Which ones were the most significant? Why?
   c. How can you better appreciate the presence of God in your work?
   d. What daily opportunities do you have at work or in the neighborhood to evangelize those you meet?
   e. When have you invited someone to learn more about Jesus?
   f. When have you invited a person to attend your parish or become more involved in parish life?
   g. What have been important conversion moments in your life? Was your conversion gradual, radical, or a combination of both?

2. **Implications of conversion and methods used in your parish**
   a. How would you estimate your parish's success in recognizing the difference between the conversion process itself, which is lifelong, and the various methods intended to help facilitate this process?
   b. To what degree do your parish catechetical methods address the needs of a person's body, emotions, mind, and spirit?

c. Is it best to use a method that begins with personal sharing, or one that presents general information, followed by sharing that connects people's individual experiences with the Catholic story? Why or why not?

d. How would your parishioners judge the adequacy of parish catechetical efforts to various age and ethnic groups?

e. How do methods used in parish evangelization provide opportunities for individual or group growth in faith and offer motivation for action?

3. **Action steps**

a. Set aside one hour a week for quiet time to reflect on God's presence in your life.

b. Arrange a prayer corner in your home and teach family members its sacredness. Encourage them to use it and respect the privacy of the person in this space.

c. Discuss with a friend, family member, or parishioner ways you can encourage those who struggle with faith to recognize Jesus in their lives.

d. Call a non-practicing Catholic and invite him or her to a parish function.

e. During the next month, read one of the Gospels, concentrating on how Jesus was present to those he met. Put the insights you learned into practice in everyday life.

f. If you are involved in parish ministry, evaluate your ministry, asking how you can improve your methods to share Jesus' message.

g. Read a book on the life of a saint, your Catholic newspaper, or other Catholic literature.

h. Visit a Protestant church service and see what your parish might learn from this church's spirit of hospitality and sharing God's word.

i. Speak to a young person, who respects you, about the role of God in his or her life.

j. Join a chat room where solid Catholic theology or faith experiences and beliefs are being discussed. Be open to those who genuinely want to grow in their knowledge of God's presence in their lives.

CHAPTER

6

PARTNERS IN EVANGELIZATION
Family, World, and Parish

When I was a small boy, Grandma put stale bread in the backyard for the birds, especially during snowstorms. Her concern filled me with a reverence for nature. As I grew, Dad and Mom read me Bible stories and taught me about Jesus. This reinforced Grandma's example from a redemption perspective. These experiences gave me a deep understanding of the kingdom of God, long before I discovered its meaning through studying the Bible.

In a similar way, Catholic evangelization begins in creation, focuses on Jesus, and finds expression in the community. This chapter proposes a model that links family, world, and Church as partners in evangelization. Evangelization happens in everyday life. It is radically incarnational, which means that God communicates through creation, history, and human exchange. Family, world, and parish are significant expressions of God's presence in our lives. In this chapter, we consider how they are part of evangelization.

Family

Because God is first disclosed in family life, evangelization begins here. As *The Vocation and the Mission of the Lay Faithful in the Church* says, "The Christian family, as the 'domestic church', also makes up a natural and fundamental school for formation in the faith . . ." (CL, #62).

The term *family* is used in recent church documents to refer to "an intimate community of persons bound together by blood, marriage or adoption, for the whole of life" (*A Family Perspective in Church and Society*, page 19). This description includes many different kinds of families—nuclear, extended, single-parent, adoptive, blended and even single persons are included as part of a family.

My family experience taught me how birth, growth, joy, suffering, success, failure, life, and death root our relationship with God. In reflecting on my experiences, I recall the words of Ecclesiastes, "For everything there is a season . . . a time to weep and a time to laugh; a time to mourn and a time to dance" (3:1-4). While meditating on these words, I remember my father's last illness.

Dad lay for months in a hospital bed. One cold January afternoon, Mom, my sister Mary Ann, and I visited him. He smiled and asked for a wheelchair. Mom pushed him to the window. Mary Ann and I witnessed an epiphany of love as Dad and Mom held hands and the sun illuminated them. The wrinkles and strain were transformed by the intense peace they conveyed. They spoke softly. Mary Ann said, "Bob, seeing them together like this is worth all the long months of pain we have undergone." This moment disclosed how deep joy often comes after struggle and sacrifice.

As Dad and Mom sat there, it made no difference that his hair was not combed or she wore an older dress. They were deeply present to one another; nothing else mattered. I saw how the most beautiful experiences happen in the simplest ways, and how God discloses divine beauty when simple people radiate unaffected love. When this happens, God gives freedom, couched in liberation from sin, pleasure, and worldly interests. This freedom invites healing and enables us to discover beautiful moments. Our common story enables us to discover these moments. Indeed, there is a season for everything. That day was our time for a beautiful moment.

People have different experiences of God's presence in family life. Often, this communication happens within a nuclear family. Many family configurations, however, differ from my tightly knit, nuclear family; but whatever the family situation, most people experience God through familial love and support. I witnessed this love in Ed's story.

Ed, a mentally challenged man, began attending Mass in a parish where I ministered. After I learned from a parishioner that he wanted to receive Communion, I met with him. Ed had no formal religious training, but to my surprise he knew the basics of the Catholic faith. I soon realized the depth of his biblical understanding and sensitivity to moral issues. He desired greatly to receive Communion with the parish community, which welcomed him. Asking where he learned his moral values, knowledge of the Catholic faith, and positive outlook on life, Ed simply said, "From my grandmother. I lived with her for thirty-three years. She taught me what I know." Ed was deeply in love with God; it would have been wrong to keep him from Communion any longer. The next Sunday, he joyfully received his Lord, a practice that he continues to this day.

Christian families communicate specific aspects of God's presence by sharing the Christian faith within family life. The family is not an object *out there* to be evangelized by the Church. This attitude implies that the Church needs to teach families how to be families. It disregards the way God is already present in a family relationship. It is far more accurate to say that families teach Church how to be Church. Family and Church are partners in evangelization.

Recent Church documents describe *family* as the "domestic church" or "church of the home." *The Vocation and the Mission of the Lay Faithful in the Church and in the World* says, "The daily life itself of a truly Christian family makes up the first 'experience of Church,' intended to find confirmation and development in the active and responsible process of the children's introduction into the wider ecclesial community and civil society" (CL, #62). The family teaches moral values, guides children, maintains religious traditions, celebrates, prays, and supports its members in ways the parish cannot.

The parish supports, celebrates, and illuminates family life through Scripture, Church teaching, liturgy, and prayer. Parish, schools, and church activities help families grow in faith and link individual families with one another. *A Family Perspective in Church and Society* underlines the interconnectedness of family members in the words, "The family is not a collection of individuals, but a living and developing system whose members are essentially interconnected" (page 9).

Parishes serve families by listening to their needs and responding to their requests. Often preplanned or packaged programs appeal to parish staffs but mean little to families. As the *General Directory for Catechesis* states, " . . . the Christian community must give very special attention to parents. By means of personal contact, meetings, courses, and also adult catechesis directed toward parents, the Christian community must help them assume their responsibility—which is particularly delicate today—of educating their children in the faith" (GDC, #227).

Some parish organizations pressure families to become too involved in activities that separate spouses from one another and parents from their children. A woman asked my advice about joining the RCIA team. Asking her why she was concerned, she replied, "Father, I said no to the pastoral minister when asked, but later the pastor asked me. I already work at bingo and teach religion classes for pre-school children. I don't think I can spare another evening a week. My family will suffer." I advised her to reexamine her parish commitments.

Several months later she told me, "I'm pregnant and decided to drop out of all parish ministry for two years. I was over-committed, and my entire family suffered. It's hard, though, because I keep getting pressure to join this or that parish activity. I now spend more time with my husband and children. We are better as a family."

Family members, by supporting one another, bring balance into a sometimes unbalanced society. Shari's story of a parent's support makes this clear.

Shari, a sixth-grade girl, came home laughing after a basketball game. She told her mom that her team got beat 25–5. Her mom asked, "What happened? Why are you laughing?"

Shari said, "Mr. Zine, our coach, is always yelling at us to work harder and harder. He told us before the game that he was video-taping us and we better do well. If not, he was going to let us have it when we watched our mistakes on the tape. I thought, he's not going to get away with that. So I said to my teammates, 'It's not fair. He's an old crab. After all, it's just a game. Let's really mess around, act like clowns, and have fun.' So we did and lost 25–5. We had a great time as he yelled and screamed. He was so embarrassed that he threw away the tape. He never knew what happened!"

The kids, sick of an adult demanding that they play like professionals, acted like kids. I sense God in the midst of this humor, clowning around in the children's hearts, howling with them at the crabby, angry coach.

Shari's mom supported her, saying children's sports are supposed to be fun. She called the coach to let him know what she thought, suggesting that he look at his coaching methods. Imagine what might have happened if Shari's mom had not supported her. Her affirmation of Shari's conduct evangelized her daughter and reflected the way God supports us.

World

The word *world* is used broadly to include activities beyond the family and Christian community. It includes work, social involvement, neighborhood activities, and cultural activities.

Such varied activities offer us many possibilities to witness God's presence in the world and to evangelize others. This happens when we urge a colleague to trust God in a difficult situation or show compassion to a neighbor. The college student who says no to another's sexual advances or the business executive who refuses a corporate deal that treats minorities unjustly evangelize by their actions.

A pastoral ministry class discussed Christian ministry in the market place, pointing out the responsibility to act charitably, honestly, and justly. Ed, an engineer, said that after a retreat he realized his obligation to avoid procedures that structurally weakened the products he designed. Ed followed through on this obligation and decided it would be his ministry in the workplace. His actions were received well and eventually they influenced corporate policy.

Jeff, another class member, laughed when Ed finished. He said, "Like Ed's, my story is about upholding moral values, but it has a different ending. I was reassigned as assistant director of a large insurance office. After being there three months, I realized that unethical practices in our company hurt our clients. I spoke out against these practices. My boss, at first reluctant to change, finally agreed. Things went along well. Office spirit improved and profits increased. At the end of the fiscal year, we sent the main office our new procedures in the annual report. Our operational mode threatened headquarters. One day three corporate officers showed up unannounced, called together our office managers, and fired us. Then, the corporation assigned a new staff to take our place. Today the office is back to the same unjust procedures that we had eliminated."

Jeff said that a Christian bold enough to evangelize in the marketplace by acting ethically faces tough decisions and may be rejected. He said parish support, lacking in his case, is very important in such circumstances. "Rarely," he continued, "do we hear a homily or witness a parish function that helps us sort out difficult moral issues or gives us guidance on them."

A dichotomy often exists between the sacred (religion) and the secular (work and societal activities). When religion is confined to church services and prayer, it becomes disconnected from the rest of our lives. This makes it difficult to integrate our faith and everyday lives. People like Jeff, seeking this integration, welcome parish support. For them, God is very much involved in what happens in the marketplace. It is difficult, however, to witness to the good news without support from other Christians.

To provide such support, a Catholic organization offered a monthly program for downtown businesspeople, entitled *Ministry in the Marketplace*. The sessions, held at noon in a corporate boardroom, centered on *Growing in Relationship With Self, Others, and God*. About sixty people attended regularly. At its conclusion, the participants gave it high evaluations and made recommendations for future sessions.

Following their suggestions, the steering committee selected the theme of *Growing in Relationship: Implications for Family, Life, and Work* for the next sessions. When they began, less than half the original group attended. Because of the request for follow-up sessions, the committee was curious why there was the drop in attendance. So they called the original members not in attendance to ask why they dropped out. Many answered that the topic was on target. If they attended, however, hard questions would be asked about their families and work, which they were not ready to face. They seemed unwilling to risk hearing God's word in the concrete world of their lives. Listening to God's word may require sacrifice, especially when hearing it means changing our lifestyle.

God's presence in the world, amidst the secular pressures around us, is an important element in evangelization. We need to identify this presence, because today's society often gives us the opposite message. Our economy is geared around money. Sex sells, youth sells, Christmas sells. The Christmas season is the biggest sales event of the year. Referring to inculturation, the *General Directory for Catechesis* says, ". . . the Church must appropriate all the positive values of culture and cultures [Cf. EN, #20; CT, #53] and reject those elements which impede development of the true potential of persons and peoples" (GDC, #21). This is an important task for the Catholic evangelizer.

Catholic evangelization challenges us to look more deeply at the purpose of money and work. These are means to an end, not ends in themselves. They serve as instruments of God's kingdom, intended to help us build the earth by reflecting God's love, peace, and justice.

Ancient peoples knew human labor was necessary to survive and grow. They also believed life was sacred. For them, the primary emphasis was on family and tribe. Functional things were secondary. Material possessions served the family, tribe, and God. In this way, early people balanced the ultimate and functional life dimensions.

Contemporary people often minimize relationships and canonize things. A materialistic philosophy of life offers a bleak hope, for humans need ultimate responses to ultimate needs, manifested in the reciprocal love between spouses, parents, and children. When people receive functional responses to ultimate needs—for example, the child who gets a new toy instead of parental time and affection—often the result is alienation. If people do not receive ultimate responses to ultimate needs, they hunger for something deeper.

Even though negative instances abound, the contemporary picture contains positive elements. Within our society, many voices cry out for justice and charity. They come from rich and poor, young and old. The Catholic evangelizer is a symbol of hope when he or she hears these cries and tries to help. There are various ways the Catholic evangelizer can try to correct injustices or act charitably— volunteering at a soup kitchen or sacrificing personal comfort for families and neighbors come to mind. In so doing, he or she becomes a symbol of God's presence.

However, we also find such evangelizers in supermarkets, classrooms, business offices, and shopping malls. They evangelize those about them. Tricia, an engineering student, felt moved to change her major to social work. After considerable thought, she remained in engineering, where she eventually made a difference in the business world.

Jim, another student, pondered a similar issue. His friends spent much of their time in inner city work. He was a math major and considered switching to counseling. But he was getting all A's and he really loved math.

I discussed Jim's concern with him. I said, "Only you can decide what to do with your life. In your discernment, remember that God has blessed you with mathematical talents and may be calling you to be the best mathematician you can be as your life's work. Consider all the people you could help if you use these talents to advance humanity by your contributions!" Jim stayed in math and earned a Ph.D. Now, he is a professor at a large state-run university, is on numerous national and international commissions, and applies his Christian values to his work.

Tricia and Jim are evangelists, influencing decisions at a corporate level. This would not have been possible, if they had not developed the engineering and mathematical gifts that God gave them. Their stories invite us to utilize our God-given gifts. The Lord challenges us to clarify our calling, encouraging us to break down the barriers between our faith and everyday lives.

God invites us to build the world in light of the kingdom. The shrinking of our world into a *global village* is a positive sign for future evangelization. The technology explosion, rapid communication, television, computers, and the Internet have brought nations and races closer together and made us aware of human concerns around the world. This promises new opportunities for global evangelization.

In coming together, our civilization can become more God-like. Reflecting on the world from the vantage point of faith, the *General Directory for Catechesis* says, "The Christian knows that every human event—indeed all reality—is marked by the creative activity of God which communicates goodness to all beings; the power of sin which limits and numbs man; and the dynamism which bursts forth from the Resurrection of Christ, the seed renewing believers is the hope of a definitive 'fulfillment' [GS, #2]. A world view not incorporating these three elements cannot be authentically Christian" (GDC, #16). These words challenge Catholic evangelizers in the world of tomorrow.

Parish

The 1983 *Code of Canon Law* says, "A parish is a definite community of the Christian faithful established on a stable basis within a particular church" (Canon 515, #1). This canon shifted parish orientation from a geographical base to a community base. Seen in this way, the parish is an established community of the Christian faithful that gathers on a regular basis to share faith in Jesus, celebrate in liturgical worship, and minister to God's people through works of charity.

The parish, lead by a pastor, is part of a larger diocese. It shares Jesus' message with family and world and illuminates God's presence in life and worship. Great variety exists from parish to parish, but basic elements are the same. We will consider these elements and how they relate to evangelization.

1. *The parish roots evangelizing activities in hospitality.*   Effective parishes are welcoming parishes. Welcomed is not something people feel because a parish has greeters at Sunday Mass; rather, real hospitality permeates a parish's style, spirit, and vitality. It extends beyond Sunday Mass to clubs, organizations, and social gatherings. Such hospitality is apparent in the way secretaries answer the phone, custodians assist people seeking information, or the parish treats new parishioners.

An inhospitable attitude is not always obvious to established community members. "We've always done it this way" or "How dare a newcomer tell us what to do" are slogans that turn people off from parish involvement. Often, longtime parish members are insensitive toward newcomers, since they are deeply involved in their circle of family, friends, and acquaintances. Years ago, after my Dad joined a new parish, he attended a parish gathering alone. After feeling isolated and unwelcome for an hour, while others chatted and had fun, he left. Dad never again went to another social there, although he remained a faithful parish member.

Sometimes, our state in life or ethnic background makes a difference in the welcome we receive. Many single people feel out of place at parish gatherings organized around parents and children. Blacks, Hispanics, and other ethnic groups may not feel welcome. Parishes need to develop sensitivity to all peoples. This especially applies to members of other faiths on occasions such as weddings, funerals, or graduations. Effective evangelization cannot happen without hospitality. It is central to Jesus' healing and forgiving ministry.

2. *The parish gives people support, in addition to what they receive from their family, friends, work, or civic associations.* Grounding evangelizing efforts in welcome, support, and affirmation is important. Often, it is hard to experience community, even among family and friends, due to changes in family life and to our mobile society. Civic meetings, sports groups, fitness centers, and work environments connect us with people of similar interests. We need more, however, as we search for a community experience that goes beyond superficial connections.

Parishes provide opportunities for transcendence, celebration, faith sharing, and ultimate meaning. They help us understand what is happening in our lives in light of Jesus' message. But just as a parish needs to exhibit genuine hospitality, it also needs to witness to community. When we perceive the parish as another organization, not meeting our ultimate needs, we may shy away from active membership. In such instances, Jesus' message is rendered irrelevant by the way these parishes communicate it.

A parish's success in evangelization does not depend on more organizational structures, finances, parish lists, or computers. The post-Vatican II parish, following *The Constitution on the Church in the Modern World*, is in close contact with society. It uses the media, Internet, fax machines, organizational development, and business practices in its ministries. Unfortunately, some parishes develop a bureaucratic style not significantly different from secular businesses. Although methods of organization are necessary in a parish, it needs to keep its mission of proclaiming God's kingdom as its main priority.

The following story depicts a parish leader who lost focus. A parish council meeting was ready to begin when the doorbell rang. A poorly dressed woman, trying to make ends meet in a difficult situation, asked to speak to the pastoral minister. Tears ran down her cheeks as she tried to tell her story. The minister, anxious to get to the meeting, gave her a few moments, excused himself, and asked the woman to return the next day. At the meeting, the council talked about helping those who are poor. Later, the minister realized the irony of what happened. The woman never came back.

Many times parish ministers cannot respond immediately to every request. But few people show up at rectories or ministry centers unannounced. One of the reasons may be that such people get the impression, "Why are you bothering us? We've got work to do."

Parishes need to reflect on the folly of planning to help those who are poor, while failing to recognize everyday opportunities to do so. Parishes exist to live out the kingdom, not play politics, build bigger buildings, or arrange more meetings. Only in the context of God's kingdom does evangelization flourish.

3. *A parish is prophetic to family and world when the prophetic spirit exists within its organizational structures.* In the Judeo-Christian tradition, the word prophesy means "speaking for God." Prophesy is rooted in community. God called the Hebrews as a community to be prophetic, through fidelity to God's call. When neglecting this call, prophets like Isaiah, Ezekiel, and Jeremiah intervened and revealed God's designs for the people. The prophets addressed the people's particular circumstances in light of God's word. Their voices challenged the established religious or social order when it was at variance with God's designs.

Jesus opposed abusive civic and religious institutions in shaping his message of forgiveness, healing, and compassion. His prophetic mission exposed false Pharisaical religiosity by challenging the people to return to the spirit of Judaism.

Prophecy exists in the parish, when the risen Lord manifests his prophetic witness through the Christian assembly. His prophetic ministry proclaims good news through the parish's evangelizing activities. Parish members witness Jesus' presence by connecting their lives to the kingdom that Jesus proclaimed. Christian witness in word or deed communicates God's prophetic word.

A parish's organizational structure influences the community's vision of the Spirit's presence. It exercises powerful prophetic witness to Jesus' kingdom by modeling his compassion, healing, and forgiveness. Prophecy is incorporated into Church structures in two ways. The first assimilates the kingdom message into the institution itself. Here, parish ministers, associations, and volunteers live by a philosophy rooted in compassion, justice, forgiveness, and healing reflected in the following story.

A community of sisters scheduled a conference at the motherhouse on Sunday afternoon. Two sisters serving in a parish nearby prepared to leave for the gathering. While getting into their car, Jimmy, a neighborhood boy, approached them. His father had died two months before. He told the sisters how hard it was at home, and asked if they would come immediately to see his sick Mom.

The sisters went with Jimmy and never made it to the conference. They could have said, "Sorry, Jimmy, we have to go to a conference, so we can't come now. We'll visit your home tomorrow." They chose serving the people over attending meetings, incorporating the kingdom into their parish and community work. Later the sisters explained to their community why they were not at the conference. Their action reflects the true spirit of the gospel.

It's a challenge for parish ministers to incorporate the kingdom message into parish life. Some ways that this takes place include:

- Always placing people before meetings, structures, and activities.
- Paying a just wage to employees. Many parish employees, including ministers and Catholic schoolteachers, receive low wages. The excuse often given is that if people choose parish work, they cannot expect much of a salary. This argument is not appropriate, for parish ministers also need money to live or raise a family.
- Putting priority on compassion, healing, and forgiveness. When parish leaders are symbols of reconciliation, their example evangelizes the entire parish.

The second way a parish incorporates the prophetic dimension is by challenging the community to act justly and charitably. The distinction between justice and charity is illustrated in the following episode.

In a Midwest city, gentrification of a poor neighborhood near the business district displaced the neighborhood's residents. After a poor, eighty-five year old man was found near death in an alley, the incensed residents raised cries of "We want justice, not charity." After reexamining the gentrification process, the civic leaders passed legislation to protect those who are poor. A Catholic activist involved in the struggle said that her parish was the hardest group to convince. She said, "The parish gives money to those who are poor (charity), but when it came to taking a stand for those who are poor (justice), and stepping on the toes of influential parish benefactors, the parish hesitated." When such a response takes place, little prophetic witness or evangelization happens. Jesus spoke a message of justice. He never worried about keeping influential people happy. Parish leaders can learn from his example.

The effectiveness of the parish's prophetic challenge depends on how the parish lives out its calling. The United States bishops spoke out for economic justice in the words, "In the marketplace where too often the quarterly bottom line takes precedence over the rights of workers, we believe that the economy must serve people, not the other way around" (*Sharing Catholic Social Teaching: Challenges and Directions*, page 5). In concrete terms, this message is proclaimed in the ways a parish uses its prophetic voice to speak out for citizen's rights. A parish's stance on this matter depends on its ability to hear God's word and communicate it.

A parish's ministries speak eloquently about what the parish really believes. When parish ministries mirror Jesus' compassion, justice, healing, and forgiveness, evangelization happens.

Partners in Evangelization: Family, World, and Parish

Personal and Pastoral Reflections

Evangelization begins in Christian families. From the first seeds of faith proclaimed in family life, God's grace begins a process of unfolding that lasts a lifetime. From a mother's smile to a father's sacrifice, God's spirit permeates a family, centered on love and faithfulness to the Lord.

In our materialistic world, it behooves us to reflect on where and how God discloses life's meaning. It doesn't come through rock videos or new automobiles, but is first manifested in the love that family members share with one another.

This love forms the basis for wider involvement in the parish and the world. The parish builds on the foundation set by the family. It provides resources for communal and personal catechesis, liturgical action, and support. Through its teaching and witness, a parish gives people the courage to evangelize society.

To appreciate the role of the family, the world, and the Church in evangelization, it helps to reflect on the key dimensions of this chapter. These can be studied individually or discussed with family or church groups.

The following guideposts are offered to facilitate such reflection.

1. **Discussing the relationship between evangelization and family life**
   a. What points or stories in this chapter helped you see deeper connections between evangelization and family life?
   b. In appropriate parish groups, discuss how your parish can foster strong families, especially religious formation of families.
   c. Discuss ways that family members can evangelize in their neighborhood or at work. Discuss the role children play in this effort, especially at school and on the athletic field.
   d. Encourage your pastor and parish leadership to go further in welcoming people and making the parish a hospitable community.

2. The implications of evangelization in the family, the world, and the parish
   a. What difference would it make if a family really saw itself as a "domestic church"?
   b. In what ways do you regard money and work as means to an end or ends in themselves? What difference does your vantage point have in the way you live your life?
   c. How does your attitude toward work and family help build God's kingdom on earth?
   d. In what ways is your parish a prophetic community? What would be the consequences if your parish lived its prophetic calling?

3. Action steps
   a. Apply one insight gleaned from this chapter to a specific dimension of your family life.
   b. Discuss with a parish minister or parish group ways that your parish can support families in their efforts to share God's message at home.
   c. Look at the parish resource library (if one exists) and see what is available for adult and family catechesis. What inspirational books encourage parishioners to follow the saints of the past who sacrificed to spread God's word? If no parish resource library exists, take steps to establish one.
   d. Investigate and take steps to establish support groups where parish members come together in small groups to pray, discuss, and encourage one another in light of the gospel. How could such groups support nurses, teachers, businesspeople, attorneys, and communication specialists in their Christian work?

EVANGELIZATION AND MINISTRY

The Gospel according to Mark contains the earliest narrative describing Jesus' call of the first apostles. Simon, Andrew, James, and John were manly, seasoned fishermen (Mark 1:14–20). At Jesus' invitation, they followed him. What inspired them to respond to Jesus' calling even though it meant leaving their work and risking rejection and death?

Before inviting these men to follow him, Jesus says, "The time is fulfilled . . . (Mark 1:14–15). The word Mark uses for the word "time" is *kairos*. This Greek word means time where meaning and purpose are discovered. It is to be distinguished from *chronos*, which is chronological or quantitative time. Mark's usage hints at why these men followed him. They saw in him the opportunity to become part of something really important, something with meaning. Initially, however, their *kairos* centered on a political messiah. They wanted to be disciples of a man who would overcome the Roman occupation of Jerusalem and begin the messianic era foretold by the prophets.

Jesus' passion and death shattered their dream, but Pentecost enlightened them to their true calling to minister in *kairos* time. This mission was more important than earthly glory and power. Such a conviction moved them beyond the complacency of *chronos* to the dynamism of *kairos*, as they evangelized the world.

Jesus also invites us to live and minister in *kairos* time. This is difficult when society places heavy stress on the events in *chronos* time. During *chronos* time, we make money, build homes, develop computer programs, and live busy lives. In *chronos* time, it is easy to become complacent and mediocre, for such time never touches the deepest core of who we are. When we experience core life events that require a response we are in *kairos* time. We live this kind of time when a mother first sees her newborn child, when it's "time" to have a serious talk, or "time" to end a relationship. *Karios* time also occurs during beautiful weddings or funerals.

We learn a powerful lesson from Jesus' apostles, who never *got it* during their lifetimes. Often, we do not get it either. We live week by week, year by year, giving lip service to our faith, but never committing ourselves to our mission to evangelize. Such complacency happens in families, who live in *chronos* time, caught up in the fast paced, materialistic world. For this reason, children and spouses, unable to find the *kairos* time they desire at home, look elsewhere, sometimes turning to gangs, alcohol, or questionable relationships.

In personal and ecclesial ministry, Jesus invites us to examine our Christian mission in light of *chronos* and *kairos* time. When *chronos* time predominates, little evangelical ministry happens. Instead, we put our ministerial priorities into money, status, functional activities, meetings, and parish organizations. *Chronos* canonizes maintenance. In personal and ecclesial ministry, only *kairos* time brings growth, energy, and life.

Reflecting on ecclesial ministry, we see how *chronos* affects evangelization efforts. Organization and management are necessary, but never inspire anyone to follow Christ. This happens in the flesh and blood witness of everyday life. In such witness, we fulfill our Christian mission.

An example of ministry in an African American neighborhood illustrates *mission in action*. Most ministries that happen in this neighborhood come not from the churches, but from the witness of Baptist shopkeepers.

In one establishment, Charissa, a middle-aged shop owner, puts aside her work and says to a young woman, "Alicia, you look sad today." This begins a prolonged conversation, culminating with Charissa asking Alicia, "Do you ever pray?" Alicia replies, "I don't know how to pray; will you teach me?"

This initial contact leads to more meetings in the store. One day Alicia joyfully tells her mentor, "I am so happy, next week I will be baptized in the Friendship Holiness Church." Because the older woman gave Alicia *kairos* time, she heard God's word. Charissa enfleshed her Christian mission in everyday actions. She set aside her daily work routine in *chronos* time to enter *kairos* time. Her actions remind us of Mark's words, "The time is fulfilled . . ." (Mark 1:14–15).

Evangelization in *kairos* time is at the heart of ministry. Besides proclaiming the good news of God's kingdom, Jesus invites us to continue this sort of ministry in our homes, neighborhood, and parish. This demands a relationship with the Lord, where *kairos* time is closely linked with our spirituality. Many distractions in *chronos* time pull us away from the interior life. The road to holiness requires hard work. As *Called and Gifted for the Third Millennium* says, "While spirituality is more and more an explicit aspect of

Christian life, 'spiritual sight' or insight is not sufficient in itself. The call to holiness requires effort and commitment to live the beatitudes" (CGFTM, page 3). Growth in holiness leads to a deeper conviction about our faith and a stronger desire to share it.

Evangelization centers on fulfilling our mission in *kairos* time, a time pregnant with the power of the Spirit. As the *General Directory for Catechesis* states, " . . . evangelization must be viewed as the process by which the Church, moved by the Spirit, proclaims and spreads the Gospel throughout the entire world" (GDC, #48).

Just as Jesus fulfilled his mission through his life (being) and deeds (doing), so we accomplish our Christian mission by inviting others to share God's love in the Catholic Church. Here, the personal ministries of individual church members converge. I realized this early in my priesthood.

Ellie, a parishioner, brought an elderly couple to Mass each Sunday. After seeing them for about two years, I asked Ellie about her friends. I had met them previously, but I didn't know the couple's background. Ellie said the man was Catholic, while his wife professed no religion. The woman's sincerity impressed me, so I suggested that Ellie ask the woman if she ever thought about becoming a Catholic. Several weeks later, Ellie called me. She was overjoyed. When she spoke to her friend, the woman answered, "Thank you, I've been waiting forty years for someone to invite me to be a Catholic."

Think of Ellie while reflecting on the words from *On the Permanent Validity of the Church's Missionary Mandate*, "Reading the Acts of the Apostles helps us to realize that at the beginning of the Church the mission *ad gentes*, while it had missionaries dedicated 'for life' by special vocation, was in fact considered the normal outcome of Christian living, to which every believer was committed through the witness of personal conduct and through explicit proclamation whenever possible" (RM, #27).

Ellie's story illustrates the heart of evangelization, namely, inviting others through word and deed to share Jesus' message in a Christian community. This happens in families, among friends, and at work. When centered on God's kingdom, our actions carry on Jesus' work. Just as Jesus' ministry fulfilled his mission, so our ministry carries out the Church's evangelizing mission. Seen in this way, evangelization is not a separate ministry but central to all ministries. This chapter links evangelization and ministry by considering ministry in perspective, pitfalls to ministry, evangelizing ministries, ministry and Scripture, and personal and pastoral reflections.

Ministry in Perspective

In a wide sense, **ministry** *refers to individual or collective actions performed by Christians for the sake of the kingdom.* These actions, carried out by Christian disciples, continue Jesus' ministry on earth. As with him, such flesh and blood witness is more powerful than words. *On the Permanent Validity of the Church's Missionary Mandate* says, "People today put more trust in witnesses than in teachers, [cf. EN, #41: *loc. cit.*, 31f] in experience than in teaching, and in life and action than in theories. The witness of a Christian life is the first and irreplaceable form of mission: Christ, whose mission we continue, is the "witness" *par excellence* (Revelations 1:5; 3:14) and the model of all Christian witness" (RM, #42). The term ministry, used in this wide sense, is equivalent to *Christian service* or *discipleship.*

Recent Church documents use the word *ministry* to refer to activities performed by Christians under the umbrella of the Church. In this restricted sense, it is limited, for example, to the work of an ordained priest, pastoral associate, catechist, religious education director, or other designated church minister. With this understanding, *Called and Gifted for the Third Millennium* states, "The lay faithful are engaged in ministries of other kinds that are also formative. They share the faith of the Church through teaching young people as well as adults; they serve in peace and justice networks, in soup kitchens and shelters, in marriage preparation, in bereavement programs, and in ministry to the separated and divorced. All these actions, when performed in the name of Jesus and enacted under the aegis of the Church, are forms of ministry" (CGFTM, page 16).

Our discussion of the relationship between ministry and evangelization does not get into semantic issues. No matter how the term is used, evangelization is the goal of all Christian service.

Ministry is rooted in our baptismal calling. As *Called and Gifted for the Third Millennium* says, "Through the sacraments of baptism, confirmation, and eucharist every Christian is called to participate actively and co-responsibly in the Church's mission of salvation in the world. Moreover, in those same sacraments, the Holy Spirit pours out gifts which make it possible for every Christian man and woman to assume different ministries and forms of service that complement one another and are for the good of all" [Cf. *Christifideles Laici,* #20] (CGFTM, page 15).

Evangelization and ministry are two sides of the same coin. Evangelization is the soul, spirit, energy, and driving force of ministry. Just as the Spirit dwells in the Church, giving life and energy, so evangelization gives life and energy to ministry. **Evangelization** *is the Spirit-filled proclamation of the living Christ, enfleshed in the Christian community's ministry.* It is the Body of Christ in action.

We are challenged to respond to our baptismal vocation by sharing the good news of God's love. *Called and Gifted for the Third Millennium* says, "Everyone has a responsibility to answer the call to mission and to develop the gifts she or he has been given by sharing them in the family, the workplace, the civic community, and the parish or diocese" (CGFTM, page 15).

As disciples, we use our gifts for God's glory and our neighbor's good. In our busy lives, we need to revitalize the Catholic custom, once widely practiced, of giving our whole day to God for Christian service through the *Morning Offering.* By our daily offering of family activities, work, parish service, and neighborhood outreach for the sake of the kingdom, we fulfill our Christian vocation.

When we live our lives in God's service, family, workplace, parish, neighborhood, and society become focal points of our call to discipleship. In each sector, the already present God invites us to share Jesus' message by our lives, deeds, and words. As *Called and Gifted for the Third Millennium* says, "The laity are called to participate in a 'new evangelization'. This means sharing the good news of Jesus personally through the witness of our lives" (CGFTM, page 12). We fulfill our vocation according to our special gifts and responsibilities. Whatever the form of our calling, evangelizing efforts are energized by the ultimate goal of ministry, which is to bring others to Christ.

All ministry is linked in some way to ecclesial or Church ministry. Without this link, distortions happen, as evidenced in the following story. A Catholic high school student told the principal that her religion teacher did not believe Jesus was God. This teacher said Jesus was a holy man, someone to follow. Upon questioning, the teacher admitted he did not believe Jesus was divine or really present in the Eucharist.

This teacher, once a strict Catholic, went through a rebellious phase during which he alienated himself from the Church, but still remained active in social causes. When it became clear to school officials what he was teaching, he was treated fairly, but replaced as a religion teacher.

The man in question taught "his own thing." His beliefs were not consistent with the Catholic faith. Consequently, he was not qualified to serve as a Catholic minister. His humanistic perspective on Christ did not mesh with the Catholic tradition. This teacher did not fulfill his responsibility as an ecclesial minister, for every Church minister is bound to be faithful to the beliefs and practices of the Catholic community. Jesus' message can be shared authentically only if our ministry is in line with Catholic teaching. In union with the believing community, we invite believers and non-believers alike to share Jesus' message.

Parishes, Catholic schools, hospitals, and orphanages help us carry out our Christian vocation by supporting our families and work; teaching the message of Jesus and the Church; celebrating Christian belief in prayer and worship; serving the poor and the oppressed; and witnessing to God's kingdom of justice, freedom, love, and forgiveness. This goal is not always fulfilled, for every act of a church organization does not further Catholic evangelization. Take the following example.

Jim, married with several children, left a good job in business to take a parish position. He knew the sacrifices this entailed, including salary reductions, benefit cuts, and evening meetings. After prayer and reflection, he followed the Spirit's urgings and accepted the position. Jim was well received by parishioners and staff alike. He was receiving positive evaluations and was doing a good job. Less than a year after beginning his job, Jim was told that his services were no longer required. The only reason given was "budget cuts." Jim was now without a job a year after he left a good job to work in the parish. Jim's situation is not unique. When church employees are dismissed without being given justifiable reasons, Christian concern does not seem to be important.

Episodes like Jim's happen not only in parishes, but also in diocesan offices, hospitals, and Catholic schools. One parish administrator, refusing to tell an employee why his contract was not renewed, said, "I do not have to give you any reasons. Our lawyer advised us to say nothing for fear of lawsuits."

An evangelizing spirit cannot develop in Catholic parishes that are more interested in protecting themselves from lawsuits than in showing compassion and love. Decisions like the ones made above indicate questionable policies, planning, and budgeting. While legal matters and business concerns inevitably enter into the operations of Catholic parishes, charity and justice must underlie the handling of such situations. When finances and legalism block justice and charity, how much evangelization can happen? Parishes need to be concerned about the negative spin-off such actions bring, when others learn about such treatment. Just because a parish is called *Catholic*, we cannot conclude that God's kingdom pervades it. A parish lives out its call to evangelizing ministry by acting justly and charitably.

We cannot excuse unjust treatment when good people are victims of poor management, political infighting, and power plays. Even when budgetary constraints, inadequate job performance, or personality conflicts require personnel changes, Christian ministry demands that tough decisions be carried out with openness, justice, and charity. If parishes fail to incorporate the kingdom into their policies and actions, little authentic Christian ministry occurs.

The same applies to individual Christians, for insensitivity and injustice also block their evangelization efforts. We evangelize by acting charitably and justly. By so living, we invite others to share faith in Jesus Christ and to accept the freedom, healing, hope, and life promised by God's word.

Pitfalls to Ministry

Two pitfalls exist when we discuss ministry and evangelization. The first pertains to parish ministry; the second to personal ministry.

Parish Ministry

The shifting ministerial focus in Catholic parishes brings with it a proliferation of ministries. This situation creates complex organizations, which to be successful require the following two needs to be met.

1. *The need for a clear ministerial focus.* Parishes benefit when they identify a common vision linking school ministry, religious education, liturgy, social action, and other ministries. Effective parish leaders work toward a common vision. An appreciation of evangelization, as the energizing center of all ministries directed to the kingdom of God, gives Church ministries this needed focus.

2. *The need to link the various ministries adequately.* If all parish organizations have a common parish vision, then the next goal is to work together to achieve the vision. When a clear focus is lacking in parish ministry, parish activities become compartmentalized. This leads to *turf* building, competition, and politics, as well as duplicated efforts. In parishes lacking a unified vision, youth ministry often has little to do with religious formation or family ministry. Without a kingdom-centered vision, parish organizations can easily be based more on a business than on a ministerial model. Evangelization has limited success when parishes perpetuate politics and competition that run counter to Jesus' message of love, cooperation, and forgiveness.

Personal Ministry

The second pitfall lies in failing to see our work in the family and world as aspects of our call to Christian discipleship.

The *Vocation and Mission of the Lay Faithful in the Church and the World* says, "The *Christian family*, as the 'domestic Church', also makes up a natural and fundamental school for formation in the faith: father and mother receive from the Sacrament of Matrimony the grace and the ministry of the Christian education of their children, before whom they bear witness and to whom they transmit both human and religious values" (CL, #62). Often the pope's message is missed by Catholics who fail to identify their service to family as an aspect of the Christian calling.

The world, too, is not recognized as a fertile field to sow the word of God. Many people do not see their chosen work as an opportunity for evangelization. For them, work is work and church is church. They fail to link everyday life with Church membership.

At the other end of the spectrum, some Catholics, disillusioned in their efforts to minister within Church parameters, shift their efforts to the world. This is exemplified in the following episode.

Elsie never had much success in her attempts to minister in her parish. Whatever she suggested in the way of outreach beyond the established ministries was rebuffed or caught in political entanglement. Finally, her frustration got the better of her. While still a believing Catholic, she now exercises her Christian calling in the world.

This woman's unfortunate experience led her out of Church ministry. Parish leaders can support people like Elsie by being open to their suggestions and inviting them to participate in an evangelizing parish. Church ministers help us appreciate our role within the parish community and our Christian calling in the family, workplace, neighborhood, and society. Personal ministry, rooted in our baptism, is joined with the ministry of the broader Christian community. Communal and individual ministry need to operate in a delicate, creative tension.

Mature Christians acknowledge their call from God to proclaim the kingdom. As *The Vocation and the Mission of the Lay Faithful in the Church and in the World* states, "God calls me and sends me forth as a laborer in his vineyard. He calls me and sends me forth to work for the coming of his Kingdom in history. This personal vocation and mission defines the dignity and the responsibility of each member of the lay faithful . . ." (CL, #58).

Fulfilling our call to proclaim the kingdom happens informally and formally. Informal activities reflect Jesus' teaching without directly mentioning his name. Loving parents, just business people, and compassionate social workers evangelize informally. Formal proclamation happens when people make Jesus' message known through catechesis, liturgy, or personal witness. Parents, teachers, homilists, and friends evangelize formally when they make explicit the message that Jesus and the Church teach.

To evangelize is to share faith. This faith sharing, also called *primary* or *core* evangelization, can take place simultaneously among various groups. It is directed to non-believers, as the Christian community reaches out to "make disciples of all the nations" (Matthew 28:19). Another thrust is strongly oriented toward the unchurched, alienated, hurt, or disinterested people who may or may not have faith. Often they believe in Jesus, but have problems with the Church. Faith sharing is directed also toward children, youth, or adults who are growing in faith. Evangelization deepens their belief in Jesus' message. And lastly, sharing faith is evangelization's constant call, inviting people to deeper levels of faith, dedication, and insight. Evangelization affirms that we have something which others seek and invites searchers to come and see.

The following diagram illustrates this multi-faceted faith sharing, which core evangelization proclaims. Within each group, evangelization proclaims Jesus' teaching, as the believing Catholic community understands and practices it.

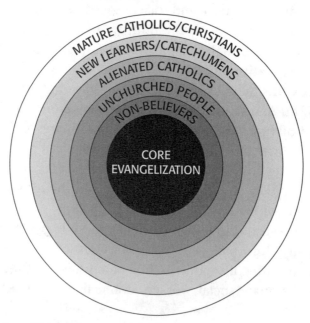

Evangelizing Ministries

Evangelizing activity is the heart of Church ministry that has as its goal the developing of mature followers of Christ, willing to share their faith. The ministries of word, worship, and service are central aspects of any evangelizing efforts.

The *General Directory for Catechesis* says, "The ministry of the word [Cf. CIC, #756–757] is a fundamental element of evangelization. The presence of Christianity amongst different human groups and its living witness must be explained and justified by the explicit proclamation of Jesus Christ the Lord" (GDC #50). This *ministry of the word* happens in a parent's teaching her child about God, a Catholic school religion class, parish catechetical sessions, adult religious programs, preaching, Scripture and religious renewal sessions, evangelizing non-practicing Catholics or inquirers, and theology classes. Each learning situation helps people understand God's word and apply it to their lives. The heart of these endeavors includes communicating the lived reality of the Paschal mystery and encouraging us to share our faith with others.

The *ministry of worship* celebrates the living Lord as central to life. The *General Directory for Catechesis* reminds us of the link between the Lord's presence in life and our celebration of this presence when it says, "Christ is always present in his Church, especially in "liturgical celebrations" (GDC, #85). Hence, liturgy enables us to celebrate our joys and disappointments as we join our life's events with Jesus' story. Baptism celebrates our rebirth as children of God, the Sacrament of Marriage celebrates our lives shared with a spouse and family, Anointing of the Sick celebrates the ongoing fulfillment of the Lord's promise to heal the sick and broken, and Eucharist celebrates Christ's special presence, as the eternal sacrifice of Jesus renews us in word and sacrament.

During sacramental activities the community gathers to honor God, celebrate oneness in faith, and welcome others. Few better times exist to show warmth and hospitality than on liturgical occasions, such as Christmas, Easter, funerals, baptisms, and weddings. Then, kind words and warm hearts strengthen weak faith, nourish belief, reconcile alienated members, and invite non-believers to follow Jesus. Liturgy is a more powerful evangelizing activity than fish fries, bingo, church festivals, and picnics, because vibrant liturgies help us appreciate that faith makes a difference.

The *ministry of service* includes activities like reaching out to those who are poor, helping those who are elderly, and consoling those who are sick. These are part and parcel of Christian evangelization. Our love, shown through service, inspires others to follow Jesus. As the *General Directory for Catechesis* states, "Evangelization . . . bears witness [EN, #21 and 41; RM, #42–43; AG, #11] amongst peoples of the new way of being and living which characterizes Christians" (GDC, #48).

If we reach out in kindness, those served may ask, "What makes you tick?" "Why are you doing this for me?" or "What is your motivation?" As Christian evangelizers, we answer such questions by sharing the way Christian faith motivates our actions on behalf of charity and justice. We need not be afraid to speak about God. Such conversations help others appreciate Christ's message and the Church's ministry.

To link Church ministries with Jesus' call to evangelize, parish and individual activities encourage people to follow the commandments, grow in deeper union with Christ and his body, love their neighbors more completely, practice the corporal works of mercy, reach out to those without faith, and welcome alienated Catholics and non-believers into the Christian community. In connecting today's evangelists with the past history of Catholic evangelization, *On the Permanent Validity of the Church's Missionary Mandate* says, "Today, all Christians, the particular Churches and the universal Church, are called to have the same courage that inspired the missionaries of the past, and the same readiness to listen to the voice of the Spirit" (RM, #30).

Ministry and Scripture

Our Christian vocation is fulfilled in many ways, including a parent teaching a child about God and a parish reaching out to those who are poor. It is carried out in formal and informal settings, as we share Jesus' message and our love. Where, though, do we learn the good news of what we must do to be saved? The answer to this question has shifted focus in the Catholic community.

Before Vatican II, the Catholic answer was "by following the teachings and practices of the Church." The Church interpreted God's message for Catholics in almost every area of their lives. When I was a boy, Mom told me that as she was growing up, Catholics were forbidden to read the Bible. She remembered a priest telling her class that Protestants read the Bible, while Catholics followed the Church's teaching. During my theological studies, the Scriptures were used to justify Church teaching. I never perceived the Scriptures as much more than a literal rendition of God's revelation.

After Vatican II, the Church emphasized the studying of Scripture. As the *General Directory for Catechesis* says, ". . . the Church desires that in ministry of the word, Sacred Scripture should have a pre-eminent position" (GDC, #127). One of the most important tasks of Church ministry is to stress the significance of Scripture, for no real evangelization happens without the biblical message. These holy writings contain the earliest Christian witness to Jesus' life, teaching, and ministry.

A post-Vatican II response to the question "Where do Catholics learn the good news of what they must do to be saved?" could be stated, "In the Scriptures, which contain God's word, in conjunction with the guidance and teaching of the magisterium." Evangelization always returns to the Scriptures to deepen its proclamation of the good news. Through reading and meditation on the word, we get new insights into discipleship. Through the Scriptures, the good news is burned into our hearts. We find this beautifully spoken in the words from *Our Hearts Were Burning Within Us*, "Through searching and growth, conversion of mind and heart, repentance and reform of life, we are led by God to turn from the blindness of sin and to accept God's saving grace, liberating truth, and sustaining love for our lives and for all of creation. Christian faith is lived in discipleship to Jesus Christ. As disciples, through the power of the Holy Spirit, our lives become increasingly centered on Jesus and the kingdom he proclaims. By opening ourselves to him we find community with all his faith-filled disciples and by their example come to know Jesus more intimately" (OHWBWU, pages 15–16). The Christian community exists to evangelize, and authentic Church witness always evangelizes. Evangelizing ministry is the only legitimate way to be Church.

Evangelization and Ministry
Personal and Pastoral Reflections

Ministry is God's salvific plan carried out in the life of the believing community. Baptized into Jesus' dying and rising, we live the Lord's command to love one another in our homes, workplace, neighborhood, and church. We get deeper insights into our Christian vocation by reading, studying, and meditating upon Scriptures.

The support of a loving parish helps us to follow the Lord. In our pressurized society, we need reassurance that we are on the right track. When confused or hurt, we need the comfort of other Christians. This begins at home and with friends, but parishes can assist us greatly in troubled times.

This chapter asks us to consider the essential role we play in furthering God's kingdom on earth through our evangelizing efforts.

1. **Reflecting on the relationship between evangelization, ministry, and our Christian vocation**
   a. Remember a time in your life when you needed the comfort of someone to reassure you that you were okay and that there was hope. On what occasions were you open to the ministry of others in your life? When were you not? What did you learned from these experiences?
   b. On what occasions did you respond to hurting people through visits to the hospital or their home? Cite instances of when and why you shied away from such experiences.
   c. In what ways does your call to evangelize mean that you share the life-giving gift of the Spirit with others? When do you consider yourself a Christ-bearer to others?
   d. What people have shared Jesus' good news with you? Are they aware of this? How could you thank them?
   e. When was the last time you affirmed a parish minister, especially your pastor? If you have never done this, is it time to do so? If you have done it, is it time to do so again?

f. In what ways do you live your life in *chronos* and *kairos* time? What are the implications of your answer for evangelizing ministry in your family, work, neighborhood, and parish?

2. **Implications of recognizing the relationship between evangelization and ministry**
   a. Before reading this chapter, what connections did you see between evangelization and ministry? How has this chapter deepened your insights?
   b. What in this chapter could lead you to take concrete action in some area of evangelization and ministry?
   c. What in this chapter could you identify with? Why?
   d. What aspects of your parish need attention so that the parish does not becomes too impersonal? Do you have any suggestions how to go about this? Tell your pastor or a parish minister about your perceptions and ideas.
   e. How welcoming is your parish? Have others reflected this to you or have you felt it? What can you do about it?
   f. What are you doing to evangelize youth and adolescents, especially in your family? Do you assume this responsibility or pass it off to the parish?

3. **Action Steps**
   a. Identify one point you gleaned from this chapter and come up with a specific way to apply it.
   b. Use the occasion of reading this chapter to discuss with a friend or family member how that person can evangelize someone.
   c. Encourage your parish to provide an opportunity during Lent or Advent for parishioners to discuss their attitudes toward evangelization and ministry.
   d. Contact other Church members to develop regular meetings in a business setting in your area for people in the work place to reflect on the pressures and responsibilities faced by Christian disciples in the business world.
   f. Form a Bible group among your friends or neighborhood people that would gather on a regular basis to study the upcoming Sunday's readings or other specific passages of the Bible.

CHAPTER

8

CATHOLIC EVANGELIZATION
Word, Worship, and Service

Welcome, support, and prophecy lay the foundation for evangelization in Catholic parishes, schools, religious communities, organizations, families, and individuals. Catholic evangelization centers around a message, which is taught, celebrated, and lived.

While assisting in a parish, I observed a girl and two boys sitting in the front church pew each Sunday. No adult came with them. Lisa was about nine; her brothers were six and four. Lisa received Communion each Sunday. Their poor clothes indicated that they came from a struggling family. Their parents were divorced, and the children lived with their grandmother. As the months progressed, I saw the kids often in the schoolyard. The girl helped at bingo.

The week before Catechetical Sunday, I announced that the religion class sign-up for children attending public schools was in the vestibule after Mass. Children's parents were to make the necessary arrangements. During the processional after Mass, I walked down the aisle, the poorly dressed children following me. When I got to vestibule, Lisa, looking at her brothers, blurted out anxiously, "Father, who will teach us about God?" Overcome with emotion, I stopped what I was doing and helped them sign up for religion classes.

Who will teach us about God? These words express the heart of evangelization. I sensed God's presence in Lisa and her brothers. In their simple way, they reflected Jesus' message and the central aspects of the evangelization process. Lisa taught her brothers about Jesus (word), celebrated God's presence with them at Mass (worship), and supported them (service). She was a remarkable nine-year-old girl.

This story invites us to reflect on Jesus, who proclaimed a kingdom of love. All Church ministries are the ongoing communication of God's love. This love is shared as Jesus' dying and rising continues. Evangelization witnesses in word and deed that this is happening. Through the Christian community, the risen Christ invites us to transform our lives and follow him.

As Christians, we share in Jesus' mission of furthering God's kingdom. This mission has three aspects: to proclaim and teach God's word, to celebrate the sacred mysteries, and to serve the people of the world. This chapter discusses these aspects separately, but they cannot exist in isolation, even though in a particular ministry or at a given time or place one or the other predominates. Each includes the others, for evangelization in light of the Paschal mystery is their energizing center.

When we proclaim the dying and rising of Jesus, evangelization energizes our endeavors, thereby reminding us of our mission to hasten God's kingdom. As the *General Directory for Catechesis* says, ". . . evangelization must be viewed as the process by which the Church, moved by the Spirit, proclaims and spreads the Gospel throughout the entire world" (GDC, #48). Without it, individual or institutional efforts to proclaim the word, celebrate it, or serve others lack the dynamism promised by the good news.

Evangelization in a community of word, worship, and service constitutes the heart of the Church's witness. As an ongoing activity of the Christian community, effective evangelization requires a healthy balance among these three ministries.

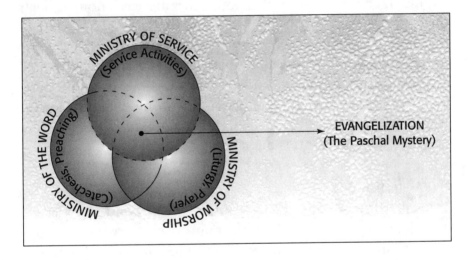

Word

Christianity is good news. To appreciate this message means discovering the power of God's word in our lives. John's Gospel begins, "In the beginning was the Word; the Word was with God and the Word was God" (John 1:1). The evangelist continues by describing the unfolding of God's revelation, centered in the Word, Jesus.

The creation of the world began a process of God's self-communication, climaxed in Jesus and continued in the Church. The Christian community proclaims the Word-Made-Flesh sacramentally and through ministries that reflect God's plan of salvation. As the *General Directory for Catechesis* says, "The ministry of the word, within the context of evangelization, transmits Revelation, through the Church by using human words" (GDC, #50).

The *ministry of the word* in a pastoral context takes various forms. The *General Directory for Catechesis* describes them as, ". . . the first announcement or missionary preaching, pre- and post-baptismal catechesis, the liturgical forms, and the theological forms" (GDC, #52). In particular, the liturgical form of preaching and the catechetical forms merit special consideration.

Preaching

In relating the homily to the ministry of the word, the *General Directory for Catechesis* says, "It [the ministry of the word] takes different forms but amongst them the most important is the homily" (GDC, #51). Then, the Directory continues, "At this table of the word of God, the homily occupies a privileged position, since it 'takes up again the journey of faith put forward by catechesis and brings it to its natural fulfillment, at the same time it encourages the Lord's disciples to begin anew each day their spiritual journey in truth, adoration, and thanksgiving'" [Cf. CT, #48; cf. SC, #52; DV, #24; DCG (1971), #17] (GDC, #70).

Effective preaching is a powerful gift to the Christian community. Homilies that proclaim God's word by connecting it to our everyday joys and struggles affirm us in our Christian life. Unfortunately, some parishioners say they do not receive support, insight, and wisdom from Catholic preaching, for it does not relate to their lives. A sign of this dissatisfaction is the movement away from the Catholic Church by people who drop out of organized religion entirely or join other Churches.

A Catholic pastoral minister received a letter from a family, once very active in the parish. The letter thanked her for what the parish did for them. Then it continued, "Unfortunately, we were not fed by God's word. After much prayer, we joined a Protestant Church, where the preaching and Scripture studies give us what we missed in the Catholic Church."

Preaching in Protestant Churches appeals to some dissatisfied Catholics, when the preachers proclaim the Scriptures in a straightforward way, applicable to people's lives. In contrast, these people often find Catholic preaching theoretical and uninspiring, difficult to apply to everyday experience.

Sunday Mass gathers Catholics in churches. The homily is a spiritual lifeline to help appreciate how God's word touches our daily activities. Every homilist, although not a charismatic preacher, needs to proclaim God's word in a prayerful, simple way. Preaching is not an exegetical session where the latest in biblical scholarship is presented. Centered on Scripture, effective preaching relates Scripture to our lives.

The readings at Mass focus on God's dealing with the Israelites in the Old Testament and on Jesus' life and teaching in the New Testament. These words, written in a different cultural context, contain core messages applicable to every historical or social era. The homilist connects this core message to our times and circumstances. The priest or deacon is challenged to address us in the context of our families, jobs, and social life, aiming to inspire us to become more faithful followers of Jesus. Preachers gain valuable help by identifying parishioners needs, hopes, and struggles. Then, as the homilist proclaims God's word, the Scriptures connect with what is happening in the lives of the people in the pews.

Catechesis

The journey of faith is lifelong. So is the need to hear God's word again and again. This continued proclamation of the good news is central to catechesis and an important dimension of evangelization.

Catechesis, closely linked with a person's ongoing need for conversion, begins in childhood and lasts until death. The *Rite of Christian Initiation of Adults* emphasizes that coming to faith and growing in our faith involves questioning, learning the good news, accepting membership in the Christian community, and deepening our *yes* to Christ and the Church through life (RCIA, #1 sequence). Catechesis is a primary means for help us to do these things.

As a ministry of the word, "the definitive aim of catechesis is to put people not only in touch but in communion, in intimacy with Jesus Christ" (CT, #3). Catechesis assists Church ministers in their attempts to "to make disciples, to help people to believe that Jesus is the Son of God, so that believing they might have life in his name, and to educate and instruct them in this life and thus build up the Body of Christ" (CT, #1). As one element in the evangelization process (CT, #18), catechesis has the same content as evangelization, namely Jesus Christ and his message about the good news.

The *General Directory for Catechesis* stresses the important link between catechesis and the baptismal catechumenate. It says, "The model for all catechesis is the baptismal catechumenate when, by specific formation, an adult converted to belief is brought to explicit profession of baptismal faith during the Paschal Vigil" [1977 Synod, MPD, #8] (GDC, #59). The directory states further that while catechesis at all levels is important, the chief form of catechesis is the catechesis of adults (GDC, #59). After Vatican II, Catholics recognized the Scriptures as essential to their spiritual formation. Adult Catholics have plenty of *catching up to do* to plumb the depths and wisdom of God's word.

The word of God is at the heart of all evangelizing activities. Consequently, the Catholic community places top priority on the Scriptures. This is especially important in family and youth ministry, for increasingly, teachers in Catholic schools and parish catechetical programs teach children with little knowledge of God and the Church. Sometimes, children of Catholic parents have never been baptized.

Some parents excuse themselves from this important parenting responsibility by saying, "We do not know how to instruct our children, because we learned very little about our faith while growing up." Acknowledging the illiteracy of such parents, parishes are wise to look at ways to instruct parents and children in Scripture and Church teachings. Many parents are open to learning about their faith, when their children are in school. In registering children for parish catechetical endeavors, adult formation sessions need to be provided for parents. These sessions can mirror in deeper ways what the children are learning. Increasingly, parishes are establishing intergenerational catechetical programs, where parents are catechized. In turn, parents catechize their children. The parish can provide an environment where parents learn to appreciate their faith and bring it into their homes. Family catechesis needs to be a top parish priority.

Catechesis goes beyond working with parents and children. It is equally important to provide opportunities for young people to learn the word of God. Many young people have not made a commitment to any Church. In their search for God, however, they are attracted to God's word, revealed in Scripture. Some Catholic teenagers go to Protestant Churches for Scripture study and fellowship, when these are not available in their own parishes. A promising movement in Catholic circles is the formation of Catholic Youth Evangelization Teams, centered in Scripture and dedicated to personal faith development and peer faith sharing.

Relating evangelization to catechesis, Pope John Paul says, "Within the whole process of evangelization, the aim of catechesis is to be the teaching and maturation stage, that is to say, the period in which the Christian, having accepted by faith the person of Jesus Christ as the one Lord and having given him complete adherence by sincere conversion of heart, endeavors to know better this Jesus to whom he has entrusted himself: to know his 'mystery', the kingdom of God proclaimed by him, the requirements and promises contained in his Gospel message, and the paths that he has laid down for anyone who wishes to follow him" (CT, #20).

Catechesis happens informally when a mother or father teaches a child about God, or when a college teacher discusses with a student outside of class how faith makes a difference in the professor's life. Such activities create a positive climate for the more systematic hearing of God's word in parish liturgy or catechetical sessions. Pope John Paul II illustrates this when he says:

> "While not being formally identified with them, catechesis is built on a number of elements of the Church's pastoral mission that have a catechetical aspect, that prepare for catechesis, or that spring from it. These elements are: the initial proclamation of the gospel or missionary preaching through the *kerygma* to arouse faith, apologetics or examination of the reasons for belief, experience of Christian living, celebration of the sacraments, integration into the ecclesial community, and apostolic and missionary witness" (CT #18).

Systematic catechesis takes place in parish catechetical sessions and Catholic school religion classes. It requires preparation and an overall plan, where participants learn the basics of the Catholic faith in a holistic way. Pope John Paul II describes systematic catechesis as a "matter of giving growth, at the level of knowledge and in life, to the seed of faith sown by the Holy Spirit with the initial proclamation and effectively transmitted by baptism" (CT, #20). He also says that systematic catechesis has "the twofold objective of maturing the initial faith and of educating the true disciple of Christ by means of a deeper and more systematic knowledge of the person and message of our Lord Jesus Christ" (CT, #19). It presents the entirety of the Catholic belief and practice in an orderly and sequential way. As the Holy Father says, it "includes especially the teaching of Christian doctrine imparted, generally speaking, in an organic and systematic way, with a view to initiating the hearers into the fullness of Christian life" (CT, #18).

Systematic catechesis takes place in a variety of settings, including classroom, parish center, catechist's home, or during scheduled retreats. It employs a methodology, referred to as the *catechetical process*. The catechetical process takes various forms, but usually it includes four components. These are the experience of the person or persons catechized (*experience*); connecting of the message presented with life (*message*); reflecting on and assimilating the message (*assimilation*); and responding to the message (*response*).

The *General Directory for Catechesis* indicates that human experience "arouses . . . interests, questions, hopes, anxieties, reflections and judgments which all converge to form a certain desire to transform . . . existence" (GDC, #152a). The Directory continues, "Experience promotes the intelligibility of the Christian message" (GDC, #152b). The catechist is challenged to interpret and illuminate the faith of those catechized (GDC, #153).

The catechist presents the *message* in a clear and accurate way. This message addresses our *experience*. The *General Director for Catechesis* emphasizes that many methods can successfully present the Catholic message, including inductive and deductive ones (GDC, #150). Through stories, lectures, intellectual explanations, dramas, audio-visuals, and discussions, the catechetical process helps those catechized to see and understand the depth and beauty of Catholic beliefs.

As the message is presented, participants are invited to *assimilate* it and see the implications for their lives. This involves reflection and prayer. The participants are challenged to see how the message is applicable to them and how it may change them.

Making the message one's own is a central component of the catechetical process. This involves seeing the message's implications for one's life and accepting God's invitation to change. This requires a *response* to God's word, which may lead to more intense social involvement, greater concern for family members, and commitment to live by Christian ethical norms in business or personal life. It may mean changing certain practices or adopting new ones. It may also lead to deeper prayer and liturgical life.

These four components of the catechetical process blend into a holistic approach, where catechesis is faithful to the Scriptures, Church tradition, and personal experience. This happens most effectively in community, where God is disclosed through the Church's faith in an ongoing way. Effective catechesis continually invites us to probe more deeply into God's love in our everyday lives. As Pope John Paul II says, "Catechesis is necessary both for the maturation of the faith of Christians and for their witness in the world" (CT, #25).

The ultimate goal of catechesis is mature faith. In reiterating this point, *Sharing the Light of Faith, the National Catechetical Directory*, says, "Every form of catechesis is oriented in some way to the catechesis of adults, who are capable of a full response to God's word. Catechesis is a life-long process for the individual and a constant and concerted pastoral activity of the Christian community" (NCD, #32).

Adult catechesis takes three forms. Each relates to an important dimension of adult life. These are the adult as an adult; the adult as a parent, spouse, child or friend; and the adult in wider society, including the workplace.

The adult as an adult

Adults need supportive ministry, apart from their roles as a spouse or parent. If they do not grow spiritually as people, other responsibilities suffer. For this reason, adult catechesis examines issues like identity, well being, solitude, affirmation, growing old, sickness, and leisure. Adult catechesis centers on relational and personal needs. To proclaim the good news of God's love, people need support from a believing community.

The adult, as parent, spouse, child or friend

Such roles bring unique obligations and needs. Parenting is a complex vocation with many challenges, including teaching children to love God and neighbor. Often, parental responsibilities and work outside of the home tax spousal love. Effective preaching and catechesis acknowledges this reality in trying to help spouses grow in God's love.

Many adults, in addition to other responsibilities, are called upon to care for aging parents. How can catechesis help them see such responsibilities as a privilege, not a burden?

Adults also need friends beyond their immediate family. How can catechesis help them model such friendships after the friendship of Jesus with Mary Magdalene, John, and the other disciples?

Adults in the work place

Adult catechesis is sensitive to the demands made upon adults in the workplace. They need help dealing with work issues that impact their personal and family lives. Take the example of Alicia, a young woman, who spoke sadly about her mother. She said, "It's too late for my mother and me. All through childhood and adolescence, I wanted her to attend my school plays, dance lessons, and athletic events. She was too busy on the fast track advancing up the corporate ladder. My mother compensated by giving me anything I wanted. Her gifts soon grew stale. The things she gave me turned me against her. I finally realized that the one thing I wanted, she refused to give me. I wanted her time, which she jealously kept to herself, giving it instead to her work. As a child, I figured she loved the money more than she loved me. Nothing she does now can recapture those lost years. I'll never have the intimacy with her that I promise to give my children."

Her mother's time spent at work deeply impacted Alicia. How can evangelization, centered in adult catechesis and preaching, help adults balance their family and professional responsibilities? How, too, can adult catechesis help people decide the right path to take in sharing Jesus' good news in the entirety of their lives?

Regardless of its form, adult faith formation centers on the ongoing process of bringing us to deeper holiness and commitment to Jesus Christ. As *Our Hearts Were Burning Within Us* says, "As its first goal, faith formation helps adults 'to acquire an attitude of conversion to the Lord' [*Adult Catechesis in the Christian Community*, #36]. This attitude fosters a baptismal spirituality for adults"(OHWBWU, page 23). In addition, adult catechesis encourages us to grow in relationship with our parish community. This involvement keeps our faith active and growing in conjunction with other adult believers. As we grow in our relationship with the Lord in a community of Christians, we see more clearly our call to discipleship, moving us to evangelize those around us at home, in the neighborhood, workplace, and world (OHWBWU, page 24).

Worship

The Christian should never be content with just hearing the word. God's call beckons us to offer gratitude and thanksgiving, and seek nourishment in our faith. Celebrating faith is integral to discipleship. This happens in liturgy and worship.

We come together in community to thank and praise God who died for our sins and who invites us to share our faith in Jesus' resurrection. Christian life is a marvelous act of praise, brought to fruition as we, united by God's word and sacrament, say *amen* over and over again to Jesus' abiding presence with us. As the *General Directory for Catechesis* says, "Communion with Jesus Christ leads to the celebration of his salvific presence in the sacraments, especially in the Eucharist (GDC, #85).

The *ministry of worship*, the second element in the evangelization process, includes liturgy and prayer. Christian worship praises God and celebrates our redemption from sin and death. It celebrates the values from which our faith springs.

The *Rite of Christian Initiation of Adults* ritualizes the dynamics inherent in our Christian journey toward the kingdom. It furthers evangelization by initiating people more deeply into the mystery of Jesus' dying and rising within a faith community. It presupposes that on their journey to God, people are on different faith levels and need the support of a Christian community to maximize their call to discipleship.

The Church roots evangelical activity in the conversion process, which points to three parish responsibilities. The first involves responsibility to active church members. Because conversion is life long, we grow together through catechesis, worship, and service. The second directs ecclesial ministry toward baptized Christians who do not know or rarely appreciate God's love and the Church's message. The parish community invites them to learn to appreciate the good news. The third responsibility initiates non-baptized people into the Church. The community helps them discover whether the Lord is inviting them to follow him by becoming active Church members.

Evangelization and conversion, centered on the Paschal mystery, are integral aspects of the one process, whereby, we come to know and grow in faith. Conversion includes individual and ecclesial elements, as it takes into account our intellectual, moral, and religious growth. The RCIA, in ritualizing ongoing conversion, celebrates a person's hearing God's word and responding in Christian service.

Catechesis is closely linked with liturgical activities in liturgy and preaching. Referring to the connection between liturgy and catechesis, the General Directory for Catechesis states, "Catechesis is intrinsically bound to every liturgical and sacramental action" [CT, #23] (GDC, #30).

All liturgy centers on the Eucharist. It plays a vital role in a coming to and growing in faith. Although it is the center and summit of the Christian life, many Catholics fail to see its significance or understand its meaning. Often, this results from failure to appreciate the Eucharist itself.

Some Catholics fail to grasp the importance of Christ's real presence in the Eucharist. Others do not accept it. Appreciating the Eucharist is a vital part of Catholic evangelization. This becomes clear when dealing with undergraduate and graduate theology students and young adults. In spite of their previous Catholic education, many fail to understand Catholic Eucharistic belief. They know something about the ritual itself, but why Catholics celebrate it and what it really means are largely unknown.

People often do not see the Eucharist as a great prayer of praise and thanksgiving. This failure leads many into an individualistic attitude, culminated in ceasing to attend Mass, because "I don't get anything out of it." These people often fail to connect the Eucharist, Last Supper, and Jesus' death and resurrection. They do not appreciate that the principle priest at every Eucharist is Jesus, who brings the unbloody sacrifice of the cross to our altars every time the Mass is celebrated. They do not appreciate that God is present in the assembly of the faithful, the priest-presider, the word proclaimed, and the Eucharist celebrated. Often they do not know how to connect Jesus' sacrifice on the cross with the sacrifices they are called to make to be faithful disciples. In short, they do not appreciate the *basics* of the Mass.

Catholic evangelization can do no better than place high priority on teaching Catholics to understand the Eucharist. Such understanding opens up new avenues of faith and dispels the ignorance that leads to skepticism and disbelief. Catholics need to know how Jesus' *Real Presence* in the Eucharist connects with his presence throughout their lives. This is especially important for young people.

Catholic evangelization needs to include the Eucharist as a key aspect, complementing the strong stress in Catholic evangelization on the ministry of the word, especially Scripture. Evangelization falls short without a strong Eucharistic component. Catholic evangelization programs are challenged to center on the Eucharist as the summit toward which other evangelical activities tend.

If we truly believed that the Word, who created the universe and every human being, is the same Word that dwells in the Eucharist, would we stay away from receiving our Lord in Communion or consider the Eucharist as unimportant? Every day, we can take into our bodies the Lord of the Universe, who made us and will judge us at the end of our lives. In unity with the risen Lord in the Eucharist, our eternity has already begun.

What better way to evangelize, Catholic style, than to help people see this great mystery of our faith. When people see and believe, they no longer take the Eucharist lightly. Then, the Eucharist itself evangelizes.

Service

Evangelization proclaims a *ministry of service*. Jesus served, and the Church continues his ministry. Christian service includes providing a loving, Christian atmosphere at home, a listening ear for a troubled colleague, and a loving response in the workplace. Church related activities, like St. Vincent de Paul, Legion of Mary, and Daughters of Charity, are service. A high school student serves by volunteering in a nursing home; an older adult serves by advising a grandchild. Service is illustrated in the following story from my childhood.

When I was a boy, an elderly black man named Ezra often pushed a small cart up the street next to our family store. His back was bent, but his eyes sparkled whenever he called out, "Rags, old iron!" in a garbled chant. In the summer, people bought ice from him for their iceboxes and sold him old rags and pieces of scrap iron.

As he pushed his cart, children often danced around him asking for a piece of ice to cool the heat of the summer. Responding to their requests, Ezra took his ice pick, cracked off pieces of ice, gave them to the children, and told his little friends to be good.

In the winter, he replaced the ice with coal. His chant became "Coal, coal!" as he sold small blocks of coal to heat homes in this poor area. When he got tired, he sometimes sat in the store with my Dad. I never spoke to him, but admired his goodness and his smile.

Each year at Christmas time, Ezra came into our store and poured a bag of money on the counter. He always said, "Mr. Hater, will you count it? How much can I buy this year?" Then Dad told him to pick out what he needed. Before I got wise, I wondered why Dad always said Ezra had just enough money for whatever items he put on the counter. One year I thought, "How can those few coins pay for all that merchandise?" His choice of merchandise always baffled me. Each year, he selected children's items, like shoes, blouses, dresses, socks, underwear, pants, shirts, and toys. After they conducted their business, he and Dad would talk and wish each other a Merry Christmas.

When I was in high school, I asked Dad about Ezra. "He is a wonderful old man, Bob," Dad said. I replied, "He sure must have a lot of children, since he buys so much kids' stuff!" Dad smiled, continuing, "You don't know who he is, do you, Bob?" I said, "Yes, Dad, he is the ice and coal man." Dad went on, "There is more to Ezra. Ezra is the preacher at the small storefront church down on Poplar Street. The church has about twenty adult members. He is not married. The children's gifts are presents for the poor children in his congregation. Ezra hasn't much education, but I know his congregation learns God's love from him. He knows the Bible and lives it, even when he sells ice and coal. Ezra is a real Christian."

When I think of the ministry of service as a focal point of evangelization, I remember Ezra. His life showed me the meaning of Christian service. I never attended his church, but if his congregation followed his example, they could have been described like the early Christian gatherings: "They come together, tell the old, old, story, break bread, and go out and live the message they heard."

Living the message we hear means responding to needy people through acts of service. *Sharing Catholic Social Teaching: Challenges and Directions* says, "Catholic social teaching is based on and inseparable from our understanding of human life and human dignity" (CST, page 1). In Ezra, I witnessed human dignity made in the image of God. Ezra saw this same dignity in every child, youth, and adult he met on the streets and touched through his church sermons. He reflected the words of *Sharing Catholic Social Teaching*, ". . . this commitment to social teaching is at the heart of who we are and what we believe . . ." (CST, page 2). For this reason we have no choice but to share and live it. We proclaim the Gospel's social mission because we believe every person is both sacred and social (CST, page 4).

The call to evangelize is the responsibility of every Christian. Responding to this call means we follow the Lord by hearing, proclaiming, celebrating, and responding to God's word. Such action is at the heart of our identity as baptized Christians.

Catholic Evangelization: Word, Worship, and Service

Personal and Pastoral Reflections

God's word comes to us in many ways. Rooted in Jesus' revelation, God's grace offers salvation to all people and invites us to respond as Christian disciples. Such a response needs constant encouragement, as we journey to God. This journey invites us to evangelize others along the way.

This chapter reminds us of the need for ongoing conversion. In our busy world, we need to hear Jesus' words again and again. The following reflections remind us of our opportunities to deepen the *amen* of faith and share it with others.

1. **Recalling those who brought you to God and nourished your faith and remembering your call to disciple those around you**

   a. What childhood memories strike you as warm, wonderful reflections on people who nourished your faith? When did your mother or father teach you prayers, read holy stories to you, or take you to church? What do such memories say to you, as you think about your children or children you know?

   b. Who do you regard in your present or past life, like Ezra, as a symbol of Christian service? What can you learn from this person?

   c. How could you take the initiative to bring God's word to Catholic children in your family or neighborhood that are not being evangelized and catechized?

   d. In what ways have you become too busy to appreciate the working of God's spirit in your life? What positive steps can you take to remedy this situation?

   e. What fault or sin is blocking you from fuller acceptance of your call to discipleship?

   f. In what ways has your prayer life become stale?

g. How would you go about finding a spiritual companion or taking off a day to make a retreat, alone or with others?

h. Under what circumstances have you become so preoccupied with ministry at church or neighborhood obligations that you have neglected your own children, spouse, parents, or friends? Take time to reflect on priorities in your life and shift out what is really important in your life.

i. How important is the Eucharist in your life?

2. **Implications of seeing the relationship between evangelization and the ministries of word worship, and service**

a. Identify a time that God's word was powerfully manifested to you? Was it at church, in nature, or during a family crisis? What does such an experience tell you about real life values?

b. What opportunities exist for you to invite someone to participate in a significant evangelizing liturgy in your parish? Whom would you invite and when?

c. What can you learn about sharing Jesus' good news from other Christian denominations?

d. If you are a catechist, in what ways do you take seriously your responsibility to be a faith filled, prepared catechist? If you are not a catechist, how could you discern your call to become one?

e. In what ways can your parish improve the quality of the Sunday liturgy, so as to feed your spiritual needs? How can you communicate this to parish leaders?

f. How would you judge your knowledge of the basics of the faith? What can you do to become more current on what the Church teaches today?

g. On which occasions are you a reconciling or divisive person in your family and parish? Depending on your answer, what can you do implement Jesus' invitation to reconcile and heal?

h. What practical steps could you take in your personal life, family, or parish to raise awareness about Jesus' real presence in the Eucharist as a central aspect of Catholic evangelization?

i. What could you do to focus on teaching children, youth, and adults the basics of Eucharistic belief and practice?

3. **Action steps**

   a. Identify what you most need to further your Christian formation and do something about it.

   b. Take the initiative to gather friends or associates and brainstorm ways the group can grow together in their adult faith lives. Choose one activity to act upon.

   c. Simplify your approach to buying things this year at Christmas and Easter. Give sacred items, like a Bible, statue, crucifix, or books on the lives of the saints, instead of secular trading cards, toys, and things that people do not need anyway. When giving holy items to children or younger people, teach them how such items are important in the Christian life.

   d. Encourage your parish leadership to develop new adult formation initiatives by studying *Our Hearts Were Burning Within Us*.

   e. Ask the parish to do a yearly evaluation of the qualities and competencies of catechetical, liturgical, and service ministers to find ways to improve these ministries.

   f. If you are a parish leader, devise concrete steps to catechize parishioners on the meaning of the Mass and Jesus' real presence in the Eucharist.

   g. Evangelization teams or individuals may wish to use the meditation on "Eucharist and Evangelization" found in the appendix of this book as a meditative catalyst or worship experience that invites the participants to personalize the meaning of the Eucharist in their lives.

CHAPTER

9

EVANGELIZATION CATHOLIC STYLE

When I was a boy, I helped my father at our small dry goods store. Christmas was a busy time, the occasion to express best wishes to customers and make the money that carried us into the next year. In those days, a ten-dollar sale was a big one. Few people had much to spend in our store. Consequently, we were happy, each Christmas, when a particular woman shopped with her family. We knew she would buy a great deal of merchandise.

Every year, she visited us right before Christmas. She always asked for my father. One year, Dad was busy, so I waited on her. I felt good when I totaled up her bill, which came to more than sixty dollars.

There was something unusual about this woman, which we noticed each year. During her annual shopping episode, she always stole some small item. While I waited on her, thinking I was not looking, she slipped a fifteen-cent toothbrush into her purse in the sight of her children. Over the years, I wondered about the impact of such an action on her children. Each year, they saw their mother steal something from our store. How many more times she stole merchandise from other stores, I do not know.

Reflecting on her actions I now ask myself, "Does Catholic evangelization say anything about such behavior?" The answer is *yes*, for Catholic evangelization considers the totality of human life. It addresses the explicit proclamation of God's word and the unspoken words and actions of our lives. It shares Jesus' good news holistically in word and deed.

Catholic evangelization is based in creation, Jesus' life, the kingdom of God, and the Church community. This chapter considers the twelve characteristics of Catholic evangelization, contrasts it with evangelical fundamentalism, and draws implications for Catholic parishes.

Characteristics of Catholic Evangelization

Even though the changes of Vatican II eliminated many traditional customs, distinctive Catholic expressions remain. We find them in our biblical interpretation, ecclesiology, hierarchical structure, ministry, sacraments, and morality. The following twelve characteristics of Catholic evangelization, rooted in God's saving love, are of special significance.

Radically Incarnational

Catholic evangelization, rooted in creation, happens in the midst of everyday life. God communicates through sunsets, mountains, birds, plants, and people. In particular, God comes through humans, created in the divine image. Pope John Paul II says that humans are "called to a fullness of life which far exceeds the dimensions of [his] earthly existence, because it consists in sharing the very life of God" (*The Gospel of Life*, #2).

Family, world, and church are primary disclosure points for God's presence and Christian evangelization. Evangelization starts in a Christian family, as we learn life's meaning through everyday joys and struggles. Friends, society, work, science, neighbors, technology, and business are often fruitful ways to discover God's presence or share Jesus' message.

The Church communicates Jesus' mission under the guidance of the magisterium. A parish, diocese, or religious community gathers us to hear, celebrate, and respond to God's word by serving others. The Christian community helps disclose Jesus' message to family and world by illuminating the presence of God already at work. With family, world, and church as partners in evangelization, God's presence is communicated in a holistic way.

Community Directed

Catholic evangelization is centered in community, not in a *me and Jesus* experience. From our earliest years, we learn about God through people. Catholics believe we are called as a *people* to follow Jesus, who himself gathered a community of disciples.

Evangelization's first witness comes through community, usually the family. We seek a personal relationship with God in union with our brothers and sisters in faith. Evangelization that stresses personal conversion and fails to take into account the community dimension of faith is incomplete. *Thy Kingdom Come* indicates the importance of community in the words, "Catholics believe they embrace the fullness of the incarnation when they embrace Jesus in the most intimate communion with his body, the Church" (page 3).

Catholic evangelization knows the Spirit creates the bond of unity, joining the pope, bishops, clergy, religious, and laity. The heart of evangelizing efforts rests in the laity, as they work in conjunction with the entire Church. Through the Spirit-given gifts of different Church members, the ecclesial community builds up the Body of Christ and announces its vibrant presence to the world.

Ecclesially Balanced

Catholic evangelization recognizes the Spirit's presence in the dialogue between the ecclesial community and the hierarchy. This balance enables Jesus' message to be proclaimed faithfully and completely. From the beginning of Christian times, the apostles and bishops, given the mission of preserving Jesus' authentic teachings, directed the Church, as heresies threatened to split it apart.

This balance between the ecclesial community and the hierarchy is important for Catholic evangelization. The Church continues to have prophets and teachers, ministering in the body of believers, under the magisterium's guidance. This dynamic within the ecclesial community insures fidelity to God's word and avoids one-sided interpretations that characterize a *me and Jesus* approach to individual conversion.

Integrates Church Ministries and Life

Evangelization creates a welcoming spirit in Christian homes and parishes. We find *good news* in our families and at church. Such news begins when we feel important and know others are glad we are present. Day-to-day exchanges between family members let us know we are loved. Parishes have unique opportunities to express similar feelings of acceptance and caring at Sunday liturgies, weddings, funerals, baptisms, and special gatherings. The way parish members conduct meetings, answer the phone or doorbell, and send out communications, speaks to the parish's belief in Jesus' good news.

Catholic evangelization energizes Church ministries and Christian activities, centering on the ministries of word, worship, and service. As the *General Directory for Catechesis* says, "Evangelization . . . constantly nourishes the gift of *communion* [ChL, #18] amongst the faithful by means of continuous education in the faith (homilies and other forms of catechesis), the sacraments and the practice of charity" (GDC, #48).

The Eucharist is the source and summit of the Church's life and ministry. Catholic evangelization is incomplete if it fails to center around the Eucharist as its focal point of unity. At Mass, the Liturgy of the Word and the Liturgy of the Eucharist complement one another. Likewise, Catholic evangelization connects Word and Eucharist with all ministerial endeavors.

Biblically Comprehensive

The New Testament emerged from community beliefs. The early Christian community gave us the earliest Church interpretations of Jesus' words and deeds. The New Testament contains the faith statements of these communities, written with a definite purpose and literary form. Some were literal accounts; others were not. Hence, we cannot interpret every passage literally. God's word was revealed through human expressions that varied according to time, place, and literary style. It makes no more sense to insist on a literal interpretation of every scriptural account than to demand the same kind of literal interpretation from a newspaper's editorial or comic sections.

While Catholic evangelization teaches that all Scripture is God's revealed word, it does so in a comprehensive way, taking into account social and cultural factors that influenced a given text. A passage's meaning is best understood in light of its purpose, primary audience, and literary form. Because these are not always clear, we receive guidance from the hierarchy, tradition, magisterial teaching, and scholarly research. We have the Church's authority to support our interpretation of key biblical texts, as we study Scripture, pray with it, and deepen our faith.

Kingdom Centered

Catholic evangelization centers around the kingdom of God announced by Jesus. Jesus' kingdom message focuses on bringing health and salvation to those whose lives are broken economically, physically, psychologically, and spiritually. Evangelization acknowledges the kingdom's presence in everyday life.

To say that the primary goal of Catholic evangelization is to *add new Church members* is one-sided. This narrow approach leads to proselytization. While inviting others into the Catholic community, we remember that God's kingdom is broader than the Catholic Church.

Reconciliation and ministry to broken people are signs of God's kingdom in our midst. Catholics reject evangelistic efforts that consider earthly success or wealth as righteous signs of God's special favor.

Dynamically Holistic

Based in God's kingdom, Catholic evangelization energizes a community to proclaim the living Christ through the ministries of word, worship, and service. Church organizations, structures, and programs assist the parish's evangelization outreach. These ministries do not operate effectively in isolation. Catechesis, liturgy, and social action overlap, even though these ministries are based respectively in the ministries of word, worship, and service.

Catholic evangelization is one process with different aspects. Proclaiming God's word is integrally related to prayer. Eucharistic actions flow from the Paschal mystery and coalesce into a holistic vision of God's word celebrated in a vibrant faith life. The *General Directory for Catechesis* emphasizes the integral notion of evangelization, when it states, "Evangelization, too, which transmits Revelation to the world, is also brought about in words and deeds. It is at once testimony and proclamation, word and sacrament, teaching and task" (GDC, #39).

Optimistic but Realistic

Catholic evangelization, while acknowledging the reality of sin, rests on the premise that the world is basically good. We believe that God created a good world and humans are fundamentally good. Moral evil or sin disrupts this harmony. The second creation story in Genesis (Genesis 2:5ff) addresses the question of evil in the word. It also promises eventual salvation. This happened in the person of Jesus, the Son of God. Catholics believe that creation after the Fall remains good but wounded. In this condition of salvation and sin, the all-holy God guides a good world and the Risen Lord lives in the Christian community.

Catholics reject Christian teachings that say the Fall rendered creation inherently corrupt. This attitude focuses on sin and minimizes human goodness. While not downplaying the power of sin, Catholic evangelization concentrates on God's grace, which offers freedom and hope. In all of salvation history, God urges people to reject sin, repent, forgive, and begin anew. We need God, for the world is not perfect—people sin and require healing.

Process Oriented

Evangelical Christianity focuses conversion around an *event* or a definite moment when a person says, "I'm saved!" Catholic evangelization believes that conversion is a continuous, life-long process. In this process a single event, such as sickness or death, can initiate or deepen the conversion process.

As we journey through life to the final realization of God's kingdom in heaven, evangelization involves ongoing efforts to discover the mystery of God's kingdom on earth. In this process, faith and good works are necessary for salvation. *Thy Kingdom Come* addresses ongoing conversion in these words, "If Catholics, beginning with their own conversion to Jesus Christ through personal reform and holiness of life, help build up a community renewed in faith, then the Church will have the vigor to seed what the pope calls "the civilization of love" (pages 1–2).

Integral to People's Lives

The evangelizing community creates an environment where people feel welcome. Evangelization begins when we are *at home*. Here, we see the significance of God's word in our lives. While at its core God's word never changes, Catholic evangelization applies it to various life circumstances. In so doing, Scripture illuminates our experiences and gives us insights into life's meaning.

Constant and Consistent in Orientation

The message proclaimed by Catholic evangelization remains constant through the ages. It centers around Jesus' teachings, as interpreted within a living Catholic tradition. Its teaching is consistent. While shifting emphasis to meet different cultural and historical challenges, its core message is the same. Based in the tradition coming down from the apostles, it is always new because the Spirit constantly invites people to apply God's word to a changing world. For this to happen, Catholic evangelization maintains the *basics* of the faith, while being open to cultural changes.

The Catholic evangelizer helps us appreciate the real *fundamentals* of faith and invites us to use these basic beliefs as stable guides for action. The consistently directive character of Catholic evangelization acknowledges that God's word and the Eucharist are keys that unlock life's meaning. Catholic evangelization provides a stable anchor in an uncertain world.

Dependent on the Holy Spirit's Presence

Jesus sent the Spirit to guide the Christian community. Pope John Paul II reiterates the Lord's presence in this statement, "With the command to evangelize which the Risen Lord left to his Church there goes the certitude, founded on his promise, that he continues to live and work among us . . ." (*The Church in America*, #7).

In John, we read, "The Advocate, the Holy Spirit . . . will teach you everything and remind you of all that I told you" (John 14:26). When we evangelize, the Spirit works through us, continuing the saving work of Jesus. We become *other Christs*, directed by the Spirit. We plant and nourish the seed of faith through our words and actions. Our efforts, moved by the Spirit, enable God to complete the change of heart. Completing the agenda of evangelization is up to God, not us.

Balanced is the one word that summarizes Catholic evangelization. This balance encompasses family, world, and church. It extends to the ministries of word, worship, and service. The balance that characterizes Catholic evangelization begins in God, is enfleshed in Jesus, and continues to invite the Church to holiness and wholeness.

Catholic Evangelization and Evangelical Protestant Evangelism: A Contrast

After a lecture on *Fundamentalism: Lessons for Catholic Evangelization* at a religious education congress many people remained, asking me what to do about family members who joined evangelical churches. Their stories about teenage children leaving the Catholic Church were similar. Some parents cried as they asked, "We are helpless. Our parish does little to encourage our youth in the Catholic faith. They feel unwelcome at Mass because the liturgy does not speak to them. There are few religious or social activities to interest them. A nearby evangelical church welcomes them and provides meaningful Scripture studies. Our Catholic youth go there. Some have joined this church."

Catholic parishes need to listen to young people and get them involved in church activities. This means inviting them to actively participate in the liturgy, ministry programs, parish council, and other parish activities. Young people look for opportunities to pray together, study Scripture, discuss their questions, and develop community. Peer pressure influences them. When parishes get them involved in group activities, young people feel at home.

Catholics of various ages join evangelical churches. The following stories shed light on why this happens.

I purchased some items at a local hardware store. Waiting to pay the bill, a man in line asked me, "Are you Father Hater?" Answering in the affirmative, he said, "Do you remember me? I'm Jim Smith, a former student of yours."

I remembered him as a fine, dedicated college student that I taught years ago. After a cordial exchange, he said, "I left the Catholic Church, when I found the real church of Jesus Christ." He then identified the evangelical congregation. Jim said that he served Mass as a boy and participated in adult prayer groups. He continued, "I never found spiritual life in the Catholic Church. My parish offered few opportunities for young people to grow in God's love. Now, I am fed spiritually in my new church." Many people tell a story similar to Jim's story.

During a trip to New York, I met a businesswoman in her twenties who described what she felt she had gained by joining an Evangelical Protestant Church. She addressed me after noticing that I was reading a Catholic book. After asking if I was a Catholic, she took out a Bible and described it as her map of life. She remarked, "I grew up Catholic and attended Catholic schools and Sunday Mass. During those years, I never identified with what was happening in the Church. Then, a colleague at work invited me to her Christian church. There, I felt welcomed and spiritually nourished. Something I had not felt in my Catholic parish. Not until I became a member of this evangelical congregation did I appreciate the Bible as God's word. Now, I live by it. The Bible gives me knowledge and support."

We should not conclude from the above stories that good things are not happening in Catholic parishes. Many Catholic congregations are welcoming communities, rooted in gospel mission statements, and committed to Christian values. Through hard work, spiritual renewal, and ministry programs, parishes reach out to all ages and socio-economic groups. Even though good things are happening in our parishes, we cannot rest on these accomplishments. The needs of many Catholics are not met, witnessed by those who leave the Catholic Church to join other Churches. They challenge us to continually reexamine our ministry.

This section does not critique evangelical fundamentalism, but strives to learn from its success in attracting people. The decision not to critique it does not imply that the Catholic Church accepts evangelical fundamentalism's doctrines and practices, many of which are inconsistent with Catholic teaching. Sometimes, these differences spring from Biblical literalism, which is not in accord with Catholic biblical scholarship.

Today, fundamentalist tendencies appeal to many people and are found in all major religions, including the Catholic Church. A fundamentalist orientation within Catholicism attracts some Catholics who seek a stable basis for their faith. Cultural and family roots that nourished pre-Vatican II Catholics are not as evident today. Many Catholics under fifty often are unaware of *basic*

Catholic teachings that their parents and grandparents learned. Likewise, strong family and social roots, giving previous generations a clearer identity, are not as evident.

Many Catholics are caught up in the pressure, relativism, and materialism of the times. They look for stability and meaning, but get few directions from secular society. Some find little security in their families and less in parish communities. Beset with job pressures and challenges at home, some feel overwhelmed by their daily responsibilities. Often their faith takes a back seat, for they never learned to appreciate the positive benefits that solid Catholic beliefs afford. Society's superficial lifestyle does not satisfy them. Hence, they search for an anchor in this uncertain world. When their needs are not met in the Catholic Church, they may drop out, look elsewhere, or move into a personal spirituality devoid of Church affiliation. Today's challenges cannot be met by the Church's return to a pre-Vatican II Catholicism. Rather, parishes need to focus on core Catholic beliefs and practices in light of contemporary needs.

Changing family patterns and job pressures influence United States Catholics in subtle ways. Religious values are under stress as depersonalizing factors enter family life. These include social pressures for elementary school children to conform to the latest clothing fads and sports activities that take children away from Sunday church services with their families. Unfortunately, some parents opt for a child's Sunday athletic event over attendance at Mass. The implications of such a decision profoundly affect a child's attitudes and priorities.

Cultural ambiguities leave people with a hollow feeling inside. They yearn for stability and a definite message that gives them direction. Some Catholics look back to a quieter time and connect with the fundamentalist tendencies found in the pre-Vatican II Church. Other Catholics, without deep bonds to the Church, join evangelical churches. Both groups point to needs that Catholic parishes have to consider in their evangelizing ministry. These needs can be summarized in terms of a simple message; a personal message; certitude, conviction, and zeal; and a hospitable community. Over the next few paragraphs, we will consider these needs.

Evangelical fundamentalists proclaim a *simple message*, namely, "God loves you; live by the Bible and you will be saved." This message touches many people in our busy, complex world. A fundamentalistic interpretation of the Bible leaves little room for ambiguity, giving absolute answers in a complex world.

Fundamentalism also stresses a *personal message* of salvation by focusing on Jesus as Lord and Savior. This personal approach connects with our quest for intimacy and holiness. It has strong appeal to many sick, hurting individuals who lack significant human interaction. Belief in a personal bonding with Jesus is a powerful one. It hints at why TV preachers attract some Catholics who watch their programs, while praying for healing. It also indicates why other Catholics attend evangelical churches that focus on Jesus as their Savior and Lord.

This personalistic orientation contrasts with the institutionalized structure of many mainline Protestant and Catholic Churches. While institutionalization is necessary to insure efficient parishes, it is critical that parishes refocus on the simple, personal dimensions of faith. As parishes adapt to meet the needs of an increasingly complex world, they are challenged to keep in the forefront the core message of the Gospel, which stresses Jesus' love and forgiveness.

Evangelical churches send out a strong signal that they believe what they proclaim, witnessed by their *certitude, conviction, and zeal*. A similar attitude is developing in Catholic parishes, among parishioners committed to evangelization. Such enthusiasm, often lacking in everyday life, impresses those searching for truths to believe. Evangelical fundamentalism reminds Catholics to be proud of what they believe by sharing it with others.

People search for *hospitable communities* in an impersonal world. Evangelical churches ground their ministry in hospitality. They welcome anyone to their assemblies, making visitors feel important. In a mobile society, reaching out to strangers is central to Catholic evangelizing ministry.

Implications for Catholic Parishes

How would Catholic parishes change if they took seriously the successes of evangelical fundamentalism? Again we might ask, "How do parishes provide a personal message, hospitality, community, stability and certitude for Catholics?" The seven suggestions, listed below, challenge Catholic parishes to evangelize their congregations and to invite others to join the Catholic community.

Catholic parishes need to refocus all ministry on the kingdom of God, as Jesus taught it.

The church exists to proclaim this kingdom, present wherever God is. Jesus taught us God's unique presence among those who are poor and struggling. This presence gives hope and a reason to endure suffering. God's kingdom offers life, hope, and freedom, desperately needed when we are broken and need forgiveness.

During divorce, alcoholism, drugs, poverty, sickness, and aging, people hunger for a way out of their difficulties. Catholic evangelization offers them a new way to look at life in light of God's kingdom. In difficult times, parish support complements that coming from family and friends. How a parish treats people who are struggling often affects the future commitment to Catholicism on the part of the people who were helped.

Homilies and catechesis proclaim the kingdom's message. They relate Christian beliefs to families and work. When parishes help us relate the gospel message to life, we better understand how daily life is where we work out our eternal salvation.

Effective parish ministry helps us deal with work and cultural pressures. It is hard to balance family and work responsibilities, which often take family members along different paths. Sensitive pastoral ministers know that over-involvement in parish ministries often takes parents from their families at times when family members most need them.

Jesus' ministry to the poor challenges parishes to reach out to people who are hurting, including those on drugs, the unemployed, and alienated people. Hope comes alive in a parish that lives the kingdom message.

Catholic parishes simplify and personalize the message they proclaim.

People had no difficulty understanding Jesus' teaching. They identified with his parables and understood his imagery of a Samaritan, pearl, and mustard seed. Such images touched their lives.

Jesus' teaching method offers important directions for homilists and catechists. Sophisticated theology and biblical exegesis does not inspire us. We want common-sense messages applicable to our experiences. Good homilies apply the biblical message to real life. Scripture comes alive when the word of God connects with our stories.

Catechesis touches people's hearts when it connects with everyday life. As in preaching, catechists take into account those being catechized. In so doing, the catechist helps them discover insights about themselves in light of the kingdom and Church teaching.

Evangelical fundamentalism teaches a definite message. Catholic catechists need to emphasize the basics of the Catholic faith. Otherwise, their teaching is incomplete.

Catholic parishes underpin all parish activities and ministries with community and hospitality.

The Gospels portray all sorts of people seeking out Jesus. People sensed that he was someone special. When feeding the multitudes, we witness his compassion and desire to make the crowds feel welcome (John 6:1–15). Today, people need to feel welcome at parish functions, especially the Eucharist. This responsibility for parish hospitality extends from ushers, greeters, liturgical ministers, housekeepers, secretaries, and janitors to the wider parish. Parishes are challenged to develop a *welcoming spirit* that permeates the entire community, beginning in Catholic families and extending to parish and neighborhood affairs.

Often, people feel like a number at work or in society. It cannot be the same in our parishes. Although the Catholic Church has come a long way in developing parish hospitality, more needs to be done. When hospitality permeates a parish community, every person—young or old, rich or poor—is acknowledged as God's child, made in the divine image.

Christian community happens when two or more people share the kingdom message on a regular basis. A parish cannot functionally decide at a meeting to create community. Community develops as people gather in faith, centering their life and ministry on the risen Lord. The Spirit of the living God provides the energy, joining people into the Body of Christ. When Christians gather as God's people and commit themselves to love, justice, and forgiveness, community comes alive.

A community-centered parish extends its arms to every parish member and beyond the parish to the neighborhood. Such a parish welcomes young people, families, single persons, and people with special needs. It extends hospitality to visitors and invites parishioners to seek ministry from the parish staff.

Catholic parishes reflect the pride and zeal that inspire parishioners and carry over into their homes and work.

Such enthusiasm invites us to take seriously our call to evangelize. It helps us avoid evil and gives us confidence in an uncertain world. It is a key to reestablishing Catholic identity and inspiring Catholics to be kingdom people. It enables us to appreciate our responsibility to evangelize in Jesus' name.

As we identify with Jesus' message, enthusiasm helps faith grow. As *Thy Kingdom Come* says, "The enthusiastic embrace of Catholicism is the way to grow in intimate love of Jesus Christ, to be personally converted to him, and to follow him as a faithful disciple" (page 2). Catholic pride begins in families. If parents criticize parish, school, clergy, and pastoral ministers, they often send a negative message to their children. If parents are away frequently from their families at parish activities, children may see the parish as the group that robs them of parental time. This does not imply that parents avoid honesty about parish strengths and weaknesses or that they drop out of all church activities. It does mean, however, that positive, constructive attitudes are necessary to encourage family members to regard the parish as an important aspect of their lives. It also means that parents need prudence, when deciding how much time to spend in parish ministry.

Positive attitudes encourage children, youth, and adults. When this happens, zeal and enthusiasm carry over to friends, neighbors, work associates, and parishes. Then, it is easy to be proud of being a Catholic.

Catholic parishes emphasize the basics of the faith.

Each parish is entrusted with teaching parishioners the fundamentals of the faith. Flexibility is the norm as parishes develop various ways to serve parishioners. For some parishes this means new opportunities for people to study Scripture, pray, and learn the Church's teaching. The *Catechism of the Catholic Church*, and publications based on it, are excellent sources for teaching the fundamentals of Catholic belief and practice.

Catechesis, especially adult catechesis, is a top ministerial priority. Today, many people under fifty have fuzzy knowledge of basic Catholic beliefs. The situation is improving with increased emphasis on Catholic beliefs on the part of catechists, but college theology professors continue to notice big gaps in their students' knowledge of fundamental Catholic teaching. Ignorance in younger years often makes it harder for Catholics to accept Church teachings as they grow older.

Parishes need to concentrate on teaching the basics of Catholicism. These include: Scripture, sin, grace, sacraments, morality, Jesus, and the Church. Catechesis involves helping people appreciate the Eucharist, sacramental life, liturgical year, rosary, devotions, personal and family prayer.

Catholic parishes put a high priority on lay leadership in ministry.

When the laity take ownership of parish ministries, new vitalism pulsates through parish life. Such ownership is necessary with the declining numbers of priests and sisters. Presently, lay people serve in parish leadership positions and parish stability increasingly rests in the parish community itself. The pastor cannot be the main focus of a parish's identity. With limited tenure of pastors, it is important to center parish stability in the people. This enhances a new *Catholic spirit* in parish life.

Catholic parishes foster a deep love for Scripture.

Evangelical fundamentalists show Catholic parishes the power that Scripture has in our lives. Since Christian Scripture came out of the Catholic tradition, it is time to recapture its significance in our evangelizing efforts. Studying and praying with Scripture every day helps us fill our spiritual gaps, as we deal with concrete realities of secular life.

Catholic parishes perform a tremendous service when they base their ministerial efforts on love for Scripture. No reason should exist for Catholics to leave their parish and join another church in order to discover Jesus as their personal Savior and to learn his biblical teachings.

The way Catholic parishes form biblically based communities, centered on the kingdom of God, varies from place to place. Whatever direction parishes take, the following are important components:

- love for and knowledge of Scripture on the part of the pastor and ministerial team;
- opportunities for parishioners to study Scripture and pray with it in parish settings and in their homes;
- a resource center for borrowing or purchasing Bibles, commentaries, books or tapes about Scripture;
- commitment to begin each parish project, meeting, or session with Scripture;
- opportunities for catechists of children and youth to learn about Scripture;
- sessions for parents, helping them learn how to teach Scripture to their children;
- retreats and days of renewal based on Scripture;
- catechetical sessions for children, youth, and adults, including children in Catholic schools, which stress the centrality of Scripture;
- a parish style that relates service functions to Scripture (for example, before a St. Vincent de Paul or similar meeting, a

participant reads a Scripture passage and discusses how Jesus' words and deeds relate to the group's ministerial activities);
- homilies centered on applying Scripture to everyday life.

Parishes are challenged to re-examine their spirit, style, and organizational structures to see whether they give people's needs sufficient consideration. This may require reviewing a parish's philosophy and planning process, and giving top priority to solid teaching, good liturgies, and service activities. A consolidated effort is necessary to accomplish this goal. This includes getting out into the neighborhood, expressing concern for those who are poor, showing compassion for those who are sick or those who are alienated, listening to parishioners' opinions, making parish functions opportunities for welcome, and dedicating the parish to ongoing spiritual renewal based on gospel values.

Consistent with the implications described in this chapter, it helps to remember the goals of Catholic evangelization developed in *Go and Make Disciples*. They are:

1. "To bring about in all Catholics such an enthusiasm for their faith that, in living their faith in Jesus, they freely share it with others;
2. to invite all people in the United States, whatever their social or cultural background, to hear the message of salvation in Jesus Christ so they may come to join us in the fullness of the Catholic faith;
3. to foster gospel values in our society, promoting the dignity of the family, and the common good of our society, so that our nation may continue to be transformed by the saving power of Jesus Christ" (pages 24–30).

In so doing, the holistic view of Catholic evangelization grows and flourishes in the hearts of individuals, parishes, and society.

Catholic parishes are not called upon to do more by way of programs and activities. The real challenge is to *be* more. This means being a welcoming, healing, and evangelizing parish, inspired by faith and the knowledge of basic Catholic beliefs and practices.

Evangelization Catholic Style
Personal and Pastoral Reflections

Evangelization is the new Catholic agenda. It underlies all ministries and energizes the Christian life. We cannot be a disciple without evangelizing. Convinced of Jesus' mission and ministry, we accept evangelization as our calling. It moves us to respond as Jesus did. Confronted with secular challenges and evangelical fundamentalism, the Catholic community strives to share Jesus' good news in a meaningful and balanced way. At the heart of our mission is the great commandment to love God and our neighbor. All personal and parish renewal begins here. To appreciate our call to evangelize, we reflect on the dimensions of this chapter.

1. **Reflecting on evangelication Catholic style**
   a. What in this chapter struck you as important? Why was it important?
   b. Discuss with a parish group the twelve characteristics of Catholic evangelization, asking how your parish integrates them into its life and ministry.
   c. Why do you feel evangelical fundamentalist churches appeal to some Catholics? Discuss religion with a Catholic who joined one of these churches, to learn what your parish could do to stop people from leaving the Catholic Church?
   d. Discuss the implications of Catholic evangelization as a firm anchor for moral values, giving a consistent direction to life. Where do people find consistency in moral values, if not in their religious beliefs?

2. **Implications of what Catholics learn from the fundamentalist appeal**
   a. On what occasions did you feel unwelcome in a Catholic parish? What did you learn from these experiences? If possible, share your feelings with a member of the parish staff so changes can be made.

b. In what ways is your parish a hospitable one? What can be done to make it better? How can you help make it happen?

c. Why do people who visit your home consider you a hospitable person? How is your Christian vocation manifested in the attitude you project to others, including members of your family?

d. How can you remedy the situation of a relative who does not feel welcome in your home or with your extended family?

e. If you get good news, with whom do you share it? How do you do the same with your faith? Cite instances of when you lived your Catholic faith with pride and zeal, or when you minimized your Catholicism as much as possible. What would help you deepen your Catholic faith?

f. In what ways is your relationship with Jesus a personal one? What can you do to deepen it?

g. Is your faith a *me and Jesus* one or do you need a community of believers to reinforce it? Discuss your answer in light of your family and parish.

h. If you are involved in parish ministry, what stories or points in this chapter are important to consider in your ministry? How can you help this happen?

3. **Action Steps**

a. Recommend that your parish set up a retreat morning to look at the twelve characteristics of Catholic evangelization.

b. After your pastor or presider at liturgy gives a good homily, write a note to him or see him in person, and tell him you appreciated it.

c. If you do not have one, get a *Catechism of the Catholic Church* and a Bible and, during the next month, begin reading them. Buy a commentary on Scripture to better understand the sacred text.

d. Take the initiative before Advent and Lent to gather a group of family, friends, and neighbors to reflect on the upcoming Sunday readings.

e. Pick out a book for spiritual reading from your parish resource center. If none is available, buy a book for your daily reading from a religious bookstore. Look for good reflections that can be read a few minutes a day.

f. Identify a young person not active in the Catholic faith and ask this person to volunteer for a church activity, like working at a fish fry, helping at a soup kitchen, or assisting in a parish work project. Such an activity may be the first step to kindling interest in the Church.

CHAPTER

10

EVANGELIZATION AND PASTORAL LIFE
A Practical Process

Parishes search for ways to evangelize more effectively. Two Church documents, *Go and Make Disciples* and *Thy Kingdom Come* greatly assist these effort by offering practical suggestions. This chapter, complementing these publications, offers recommendations for parish evangelization. It is divided into three sections: evangelization's goal of proclaiming God's good news of salvation, the importance of knowing and responding to people's needs, and practical ways for a parish to proceed.

Proclaiming God's Good News of Salvation

Evangelization begins by acknowledging God's presence in life. Creation's mystery hints at God's love, beauty, and compassion. At the same time, creation reflects struggle, sorrow, and death. All great religious traditions try to reconcile the ambiguities in our wonderful, yet broken world.

Christian evangelization faces human paradoxes in light of Jesus' life and teachings. A Christian evangelist's first responsibility is to know Jesus' message. This means that parish evangelization needs to emphasize the Scriptures. Other aspects of Christian evangelization rest upon God's revealed word. Once we appreciate this word, we become more enthusiastic about sharing it.

Catholic evangelization interprets God's word in light of the Catholic tradition. Since the New Testament flowed from early community beliefs, tradition guides their interpretation, insuring that the Church remains faithful to Jesus' teaching. In this regard, we are reminded that the "ministry of evangelization does not consist in following a recipe, but in letting the Spirit open our hearts to God's word so that we can live and proclaim God's word to others" (*Go and Make Disciples*, page 22).

The most basic principle of Catholic evangelization is *stress Scripture and help people understand Jesus' message, so they can apply it to their lives and share it with others*. This begins in the family and is fostered in the parish. If Catholics do not give high priority to this principle, parish renewal has only limited success. People need to know God's word for Catholic evangelization to bear fruit.

Knowing People's Needs and Responding to Them

A parish catechetical team asked me to be a consultant for their youth religious education program. The team included seven well-prepared catechists, sincerely interested in their ministry. They developed a catechetical program and advertised it. The syllabus, teachers, and support staff were in place. The first evening, with seven catechists ready to teach, no young people came.

As we discussed their problem, it became clear that neither the program nor the time fit the students' needs. Every week, fifty teenagers, who attended different public schools, came to the parish to play volleyball and basketball on the evening before the scheduled religion classes. Following our meeting, the catechetical staff solicited input from the students and their parents. After discussing the issue with them on several occasions, all agreed to merge catechesis, socials, and sports into a total youth ministry program.

Parish ministerial efforts need to connect with our everyday lives. In speaking of the goals of evangelization, *Go and Make Disciples* says, "These goals must bear upon our *everyday life*, in the family and the workplace, in the way we live . . . all evangelization planning basically strives to make more possible the kind of everyday exchange between believers and unbelievers which is the thrust of evangelization" (page 22). As this pertains to youth, it reminds parishes to connect evangelization and catechetical efforts to the actual situation of young peoples' lives. When people do this, youth usually listen and respond.

Parish evangelization has limited results if people's needs are not met. The first requirement for successful parish evangelization is to ascertain people's needs, illustrated in the following story.

When the population of a southwestern United States town shifted to predominantly poor Mexican Americans, the Catholic parish continued to operate with a white-Anglo mentality. The pastor and parish ministers were rarely seen in the neighborhood. But evangelical preachers and their parishioners knocked on doors and invited the immigrants to visit their churches. Most new neighborhood residents did not speak English. Many had little money and all feared for their families. Even with roots firmly planted in the Catholic tradition, they left the Catholic Church because evangelical churches welcomed them, spoke their language, and met their needs.

People's needs vary from area to area, parish to parish, family to family. Consequently, it is a mistake to believe that one blueprint addresses all evangelization needs. Only after a parish appreciates its member's physical, psychological, and spiritual needs can it effectively meet these needs.

Parish ministers reach people by appealing to their core or depth dimension. Everyone searches for meaning, everyone suffers, and everyone needs deliverance. Since these realities underlie all evangelization efforts, the first prerequisite for successful evangelization is making people feel important and welcome.

While keeping people's needs in the forefront and acknowledging the importance of welcome, parishes should remember three presuppositions for success in parish evangelization: evangelization is not a separate ministry, evangelization demands personal presence, and evangelization is rooted in Scripture and shared faith.

Not a Separate Ministry

Over-organization and specialization of ministries often leads to irresponsibility. When this happens, the youth minister may say, "Catechesis is not my responsibility; it's the job of the parish school of religion." The adult education coordinator may conclude, "I'm not required to work with senior adults. That is the job of the person hired to minister to the aged." In situations like this, it's not surprising to hear people say, "Evangelization? Oh, there's a special team to do that work."

Since evangelization is not a separate ministry but is an integral aspect of all ministries, the pastor is the center of every evangelization effort. Even if he designates someone else to oversee its practical planning, he still needs to insure that all parish ministries support evangelization and incorporate it into their work.

Go and Make Disciples reiterates this holistic approach to parish evangelization when it states, ". . . an evangelizing spirit will touch every dimension of parish life. Welcome, acceptance, the invitation to conversion and renewal, reconciliation and peace, beginning with our worship, must characterize the whole tenor of our parishes. Every element of the parish must respond to the evangelical imperative—priests and religious, laypersons, staff, ministers, organizations, social clubs, parochial schools, and parish religious education programs" (page 23).

Personal Presence

When a newly appointed pastor first offered the Sunday liturgy in an African American, inner-city parish, sixty-seven people attended. The next day, he began knocking on doors in the neighborhood. For six months, he went house to house. His message in every place was the same. "Hi, I'm Father Jim, the new pastor of St. Ben's. Can I visit your home?" After spending time with each household, he left with the words, "I appreciate your hospitality. Now I invite you to my home. Stop and see me at the rectory, and I'll show you where I live." Ten years later, when Father Jim left that parish, over six hundred people attended his farewell Mass and wished him a tear-filled, yet happy good-bye.

Father Jim's story reflects Jesus' way. He walked the dusty roads of Galilee and Judea, healing people, visiting homes, and forgiving sinners. Jesus went where people were. So did Father Jim. So must every evangelizer.

And yet, being around people isn't enough. The evangelizer is challenged to be really present. This means making people feel important and listening to their unspoken words and feelings. Personal presence means taking time with others. When an evangelizer gives time to another, it has a tremendous impact. Evangelization's success often rests on the time Catholics give to one another.

Centrality of Scripture and Faith Sharing

More is required than personal presence for successful evangelization. The evangelist's primary function is to share faith with those who do not profess belief in Jesus Christ. *Evangelization in the Modern World* says, "To reveal Jesus Christ and His Gospel to those who do not know them has been, since the morning of Pentecost, the fundamental program which the Church has taken on as received from her founder" (#51).

Hence, the heart of evangelization is sharing faith with those who do not believe. Pope Paul VI stated, "The Good News proclaimed by the witness of life sooner or later has to be proclaimed by the word of life. There is no true evangelization if the name, the teaching, the life, the promises, the kingdom and the mystery of Jesus of Nazareth, the Son of God are not proclaimed" (*Evangelization in the Modern World*, #22).

Jesus calls us to proclaim the gospel. For the mature Christian, evangelization is the full expression of what it means to be a Christian.

Practical Ways for a Parish to Proceed

A goal of every parish is to help parishioners realize their part in Catholic evangelization. This includes outreach to church members, alienated Catholics, and unchurched people. Any pastoral plan for evangelization implies two dynamics: spiritual renewal and shared faith.

Because parishes differ in size, location, leadership, ethnic mix, parishioner mobility, and needs, evangelization models differ according to local circumstances. At the same time, certain suggestions help parishes develop effective evangelization. This section considers where to begin, how to proceed, and what pitfalls to avoid.

Where to Begin

Thy Kingdom Come offers valuable insights into the centrality of parish evangelization. We read, "Since evangelization is the essential mission of the Church and parish is the Church present in a given place, all parishes should have evangelization teams, or at least individual evangelizers, working closely with the pastor, council, and staff. An evangelization team is not a luxury or an addition, but a part of normal parish planning, normal parish life. Making this fundamental point to the pastor and parish leadership is perhaps the most important act of evangelization diocesan designates perform. The long-term effectiveness of their ministry depends on how successfully they can move evangelization from the 'take-it-or-leave-it' margin to the 'must-do' core" (page 9).

Parish evangelization begins by looking to Jesus for guidance. He began his public ministry by calling a few disciples and teaching them his message. Following in Jesus' footsteps, parish evangelization often begins with someone taking a leadership role and inviting several parishioners to join an evangelization effort. The initiative for evangelization may begin with the pastor, but it can come from a parishioner, who proceeds with his approval. Without the pastor's blessing, evangelization has limited success. The following steps suggest a way to begin.

1. Designate a parish evangelization coordinator. This person can be someone already interested in and knowledgeable about evangelization, or a person enthusiastic and capable of learning about evangelization and coordinating small groups.
2. Identify parishioners willing to probe the meaning of evangelization in personal and parish life. The parishioners selected, usually four to seven, are called the *evangelization team* or something similar. This team does not do all the one-on-one evangelization but discerns ways that the parish as-a-whole can effectively evangelize. The team exercises an overseeing role. It is not responsible for all the parish's evangelization!

Referring to the selection of evangelization team members, *Thy Kingdom Come* states, "The pastor should take a very active role in this discernment, since he will be working very closely with parish team members as they carry out their mission. In general, the parish evangelization team will include active Catholics with a real enthusiasm for their faith and the ability to draw people into the love of Jesus and the Catholic way of life" (pages 9–10).

3. Decide the most effective way for the evangelization team to begin. Preparation for its ministry includes prayer and discernment. *Thy Kingdom Come* reiterates the importance of team preparation saying, "Formation should involve prayer, spirituality, in-depth Scripture study, practice in community-building, an analysis of the state of the local church, and an overview of Catholic teaching, including church history" (page 10).

A big temptation for any newly formed evangelization team to avoid is the need to produce immediate results. The team cannot succumb to this heresy in action, but must take time to ascertain how the Holy Spirit invites this particular parish to evangelize. Several suggestions help facilitate this process;

- Begin with a day of prayer or retreat.

- Center weekly group meetings on prayer, Scripture, and Church teachings on evangelization. The agenda of team meetings should include reflecting on how Jesus and his disciples evangelized by studying the New Testament and learning various dimensions of Catholic evangelization by reading Church instructions on evangelization, especially Pope Paul VI's *Evangelization in the Modern World*. Without a solid biblical base, the evangelization team can get sidetracked by the numbers game, competition, or exclusivity. Without a grounding in Church documents, the evangelization team can miss its link with the larger ecclesial community. The team needs to spend time, maybe as much as several months, preparing for its ministry through prayer, study, and reflection.
- As the team comes to appreciate Jesus' evangelizing message, it asks, "How can this message best be applied in our parish? What are the parishioner's needs?"
- When the team identifies its focus, the pastor's role becomes more important. If he is not a member of the team, he is invited to join, for the pastor is the chief parish evangelizer. If he chooses not to join the team, he is kept informed and supports what is happening.

How to Proceed

After the evangelization team prepares through prayer, learning, and discernment, it invites the Catholic community to become an evangelizing parish. *Thy Kingdom Come* says, "The team's first job, then, is evangelization of the parish community itself. However, the team also initiates and guides the parish' missionary outreach to inactive Catholics and the unchurched" (page 11). No single model exists to accomplish this, but certain points are clear.

1. The process begins by eliciting the pastor's cooperation and leadership. This is critical. The pastor's personal support, liturgical ministry of preaching, catechetical responsibilities, and administrative decisions on hiring personnel and allocating parish funds affect the success of parish evangelization.

2. The next step is to approach various parish leaders and invite them to make a commitment to evangelization. These leaders include any of the following people who may be employed or volunteer in the parish: the school principal, religious education director, parish council president, finance committee chairperson, St. Vincent de Paul coordinator, liturgical director, and youth minister. These people need to understand their role in raising the awareness of a parish's evangelical responsibilities. Only after Church leaders acknowledge the entire parish's responsibility to evangelize, does evangelization succeed.

As this process occurs, a decision is made to hire, or accept as volunteers, for parish ministerial jobs only those people who are committed to evangelization. Likewise, only parish members who accept the parish's call to evangelize serve in parish leadership roles, such as the education committee, parish council, athletic board, and finance committee. The latter committee must be convinced of the parish's commitment to evangelization. Otherwise, monies are easily spent on misplaced parish priorities.

Generally, an evangelizing parish does not need new committees or organizational structures. In an evangelizing parish, people in existing organizations accept their responsibility to evangelize the parish community to its role in proclaiming Jesus' good news.

3. The final step involves actual outreach by church leaders to the broader parish population. In this process, the evangelization team supports and advises various parish committees and leaders, who, in turn, evangelize church members. Several recommendations may help.
   • The pastoral team, including the pastor and parish staff, formulates a practical parish evangelization plan. Responsibility to develop this plan can be given to the evangelization team, which submits its recommendations to the pastoral team for modification and approval.
   • The pastoral plan accounts for parish needs, such as evangelizing youth, reconciling alienated Catholics, and

reaching out to unchurched people. In addition, it includes ways that parish leaders and organizations cooperate in whatever plan is established. It also suggests ways for church members see their responsibility to evangelize. Finally, it establishes a timetable and an ongoing method of evaluation.

- A mission or spiritual renewal initiates the wider parish into its role in the evangelization process. Every parish leader communicates the parish evangelization plan to his or her organization. The cooperation of parish council members, schoolteachers, catechists, choir members, servers, ushers, coaches, and such like is necessary. This commitment to evangelization is ongoing, even as parish personnel change. The pastor reiterates the parish's evangelization commitment in homilies, and as he encourages parishioners to extend welcome in the liturgy, meetings, and parish socials.

- As the evangelization thrust gets out to parish members through homilies, announcements, encouragement of parish leaders, youth groups, and parish organizations, opportunities are provided for parishioners to learn more about Scripture, Church teachings and prayer. Catholics come to see themselves as evangelizers in their homes, with friends, among alienated Catholics, with the unchurched, in their neighborhoods, and with the civic community. A feedback system is set up between parishioners and parish leaders to reach needy people and to contact potential parish members.

The goal of the process is to call the entire parish to evangelize. As the evangelization movement builds, the evangelization team responds by preparing new evangelizers. *Thy Kingdom Come* speaks of training evangelists for ministries, ". . . like home visitation, or at least directing them to training opportunities. It provides focus and leadership within the community, so that parishioners who want to live out their baptismal call to evangelize know where to turn to get the proper skills" (page 11).

Pitfalls to Avoid

First and foremost, parishes should avoid the pitfall of presenting evangelization as a new program. Evangelization is what Christian life is about; namely, witness, concern and love. With this in mind, the following suggestions are offered.

1. *Avoid clannishness.* After Vatican II, some parish renewal deteriorated into clannishness. If people, active in renewal programs, gave the impression of superiority, parishioners may have felt pressured to participate in renewal to be accepted by the parish in-crowd. Evangelization teams cannot fall into a similar trap of thinking they are special. If this happens, little cooperation takes place among parish members.

2. *Be open and ongoing.* Since parish evangelization is a process not a product, it is open and ongoing. As parishioners change and leadership changes, accommodations have to be made.

3. *Avoid Institutionalization.* Parish evangelization cannot become one program among many, nor can it be viewed as a separate ministry. It is central to all ministries. Among other things, this means that a separate evangelization budget does not have to be set up. Monies allocated for evangelization are directed through already-existing parish organizations. For example, the appropriate catechetical, liturgical, service, and youth ministers budget monies for bibles, books, tapes, and funds for the poor.

4. *Do not base evangelization on money.* Evangelization's success rests on people, not money. A parish leader recently said, "We can't do much evangelization, because we are a poor parish with little money." Seen from a biblical perspective, another reply is forthcoming. We are limited creatures, and God's Spirit evangelizes through our strengths and brokenness. We do not need expensive programs, speakers, and media ads to share who we are as followers of Christ.

5. *Do not over-structure.* To accomplish its evangelical mission, parish ministries identify people's needs, organize renewal efforts, and reach out to alienated Catholics or unchurched people. As this happens, room is left for the spontaneous workings of the Holy Spirit. When too much bureaucracy exists, structures can become more important than evangelization itself.

6. *Revolve leadership.* Every parish has parishioners who have been *in charge* of this or that task for years. They work in the rectory, coordinate church functions, direct the choir, or run various parish organizations. Their loyalty is commendable, but their motivation is questionable, if they block other leaders from emerging or refuse to turn over responsibilities to them.

Parish evangelization works well with a revolving leadership process. This is accomplished through a limited commitment, possibly three-years. During the first year, person *A* is in charge, with person *B* learning the job as an apprentice. In the second year, person *B* takes over the leadership and person *C* becomes the apprentice, while person *A* acts as an ad-hoc consultant to person *B*. In the third year, person *B* acts as a consultant to person *C*. This process insures continuity and fresh leadership.

The objective of all parish ministries is to form Christians who acknowledge their vocation to share faith. Evangelizers help the broader church community to see this calling. A parish reinvigorates its ministries through evangelization, which invites parishioners to acknowledge their concern for friends, enemies, and all people.

Let our lives reflect the words of *Thy Kingdom Come* as we accept our baptismal call to evangelize, "Having been sent out and evangelized, the Church herself sends out evangelizers. She puts on their lips the saving Word, she explains to them the message of which she herself is the depositary, she gives them the mandate which she herself has received and sends them out to preach . . . There is thus a profound link between Christ, the Church, and evangelization. During the period of the Church that we are living in, it is she who has the task of evangelizing. This mandate is not accomplished without her, and still less against her" (EMW, #s 15–16).

Only in collaboration with the mission of Jesus and the Church do we evangelize most fully. This is our call as disciples of Jesus Christ.

Evangelization and Pastoral Life: A Practical Process

Personal and Pastoral Reflections

The Good News of Jesus Christ bears little fruit without disciples who share it, for the ongoing incarnation of Jesus' message happens through us. This is an awe-inspiring task, requiring faith and humility. God calls us to share this message with family members, friends, neighbors, the Church community, and those who do not know Jesus.

This formidable task begins in the simplest ways—the love of a parent or friend, the sacrifice of a teacher or social worker, and the dedication of a church minister. Evangelizing society requires a personal commitment and preparation on the part of those engaged in ministerial activities. This chapter offers tips to begin and further this process. The following suggestions provide further opportunities for reflection and action.

1. **Reflecting on evengelization and parish life**
   a. How do you prepare yourself for your calling as a disciple of Jesus Christ, invited to further his good news?
   b. Give an example of a time you were evangelized by someone and a time that you needed evangelization, but no one was there. What can you learn from these experiences?
   c. Describe an occasion when you felt personally present to someone who needed you; a time when someone was present to you in similar circumstances; a time when you needed someone with you, but there was no one. What do these experiences tell you about the relationship between evangelization and personal presence? How do insights from the above situations affect your attitude toward evangelizing in ordinary life?
   d. In this chapter, what stories or statements from Church documents struck you? Why? What practical consequences do they imply for your life and ministry or that of your parish?

2. **Implications of evangelization and parish life**
   a. What concrete difference would it make if parishes saw themselves as evangelizing communities? How would this realization affect the quality of parish hospitality and welcome?
   b. Has your parish made a serious effort to develop leadership among youth, as this pertains to giving them the knowledge and skills to share their faith with others? What could you do to initiate a youth evangelization team in your parish? How would such a team be received?
   c. What up-to-date Church documents or other writings on evangelization does your parish library or resource room have? How can these be advertised, so parish members use them? If they are not available, what can be done to obtain them?
   d. How could a retreat or mission centered on evangelization help your parish grow in faith and holiness?
   e. Discuss whether the people in your neighborhood consider your parish as a place where they are welcome. How does their overall response to your parish link with the need to make your parish a welcoming and evangelizing community?

3. **Action Steps**
   a. Reflect on points in this chapter that spoke most clearly to you and make one concrete resolution as a result of your reflections.
   b. Discuss, with a parish minister or at parish council, the state of evangelization in your parish. Encourage the parish, if it does not have one, to form an evangelization team.
   c. Read *On Evangelization in the Modern World, Thy Kingdom Come, Go and Make Disciples* or a similar book to further your insights into the evangelization process.

d. Select one of the Gospels, read it, and reflect on how Jesus' response to people in this Gospel gives you insights into evangelization. If possible, do this in a prayer or study group with other parishioners.
e. Encourage your pastor to preach evangelizing homilies, bringing the call to discipleship into homilies whenever possible.
f. Recommend that evangelization becomes a parish priority during the coming year.

Conclusion

It's winter now and snowflakes fall outside my window. Soon, spring will come, and the robin I heard as I began this book on Catholic evangelization will return.

I remember the robin's song, with its echo of new life, God's love and memories of my own story. My story is every person's story, told in different times and places. Human stories only make sense when they are faithful to God's story. I hope this book has encouraged you to share Jesus' good news through your stories.

Evangelization is every Christian's vocation. The parish furthers this vocation through the ministries of welcome, word, worship, and service. In so doing, it invites all people—young and old, rich and poor, black, yellow, red, brown and white—to join their hands and hearts and walk boldly into God's kingdom.

APPENDIX

EUCHARIST AND EVANGELIZATION

"*O*h, Bob! You should have seen the beautiful sunset this morning, as I sat in my chair and looked over the fields beyond our back yard." The power of God's beauty, disclosed in a sunset spoke *good news* to my eighty-nine year old Mother, as she sat with Hannah, her dog.

The spot where Mom sat was four feet from one of the most powerful liturgies I have ever experienced. It happened the Sunday after my father died, nineteen years ago around our family dining room table, with my mother and me sitting beside one another. We were alone, except for the sun that streamed through the same window that inspired Mom's comments about the beautiful sunset.

I remember that Sunday morning like it was yesterday. Mom and I grieved deeply over Dad's death as we prepared for our Eucharistic celebration. The readings and prayers conveyed unusual power that morning, as we reflected in our hearts and with our voices about Dad's life and goodness. When I received the Eucharist, a profound awareness of the transcendence of God overcame me. As I looked at Mom, I felt the warmth of the sun on my face, and remembered the happy and sad times that we celebrated as a family in this very spot.

At that moment, the Risen Lord became incarnate again in the flesh and blood experience with the person I most loved in this world. We became one with my father in the communion of saints, overcome by joy and gratitude that comes from faith. As I looked at Mom, her eyes were closed in prayer. Seeing her, I knew she had also experienced a similar transcendent moment in the panorama of life beyond my father's death.

In reflecting on the words of my mother about the beautiful sunset and the liturgical experience after Dad's death, I saw the connection between evangelization and the Eucharist.

Evangelization

Four key components of God's self-communication, described in terms of evangelization or sharing the good news of God's love, manifested themselves through the sunset experience and liturgical celebration at our dining room table. These components are nature, human community, faith, and ritual.

Nature

Pope Paul VI in *On Evangelization in the Modern World* describes evangelization as "bringing the Good News into all the strata of humanity, and through its influence transforming humanity from within and making it whole" (EN, #18). In Catholic theology creation was wounded, not corrupted, after the fall of Adam. Hence, God is first manifested in creation. My mother reflected this reality in her description of the beautiful sunset.

The first communication of a transcendent, loving God comes in creation, which roots all evangelization efforts. Current environmental concerns help us identify God's presence in creation. We witness nature's dying and rising, as we experience the change of seasons, stages of the moon, the rising and setting of the sun, and the birth of a child. Appreciating God's activity in redemption means understanding its foundation in creation.

For many people, finding God in creation is concurrent with appreciating God's workings in loving human interchanges and in Jesus. Witnessing the Lord in others often leads us to Jesus. "Communion with Jesus Christ leads to the celebration of his salvific presence in the sacraments, especially the Eucharist" (GDC, #85). Without this link between human and divine love, sacramental activities, especially the Eucharist, are incomplete and have limited impact. Celebrating the Eucharist around our table with Mom brought the brokenness we experienced through my father's death into direct contact with the brokenness of Christ on the cross, which we celebrated at Mass. The Mass continues the eternal sacrifice of the cross, culminating in Jesus' resurrection. The Paschal mystery promises liberation from sorrow, sin, and death. Sitting with Mom that morning reminded me that "the humble and poor are evangelized, become his disciples, and gather together 'in his name' in the great community of those who believe in him. . . . Thus he accomplishes his revelation . . . by signs and miracles, and more especially by his death, by his resurrection, and by the sending of the Spirit of Truth" (EN, #12).

Human Communication

As Mom and I sat at the table, our love for Dad and the deep recognition of his being gone enhanced Jesus' Eucharistic presence. In our world, God's presence is first disclosed in creation and in people of good will. God's revelation to the Hebrews culminated in Jesus' incarnation (his birth, life, dying, and rising). Today, his incarnation continues through the Risen Lord's presence in the Christian community.

In its most basic form, a Christian community begins in the family, the domestic church, which Mom and I celebrated that Sunday morning. In referring to the domestic church, Pope Paul VI says, "This means that there should be found in every Christian family the various aspects of the entire Church . . . The family, like the Church, ought to be a place where the Gospel is transmitted and from which the Gospel radiates" (EN, #71). Because this happened over our family's lifetime, Mom and I could share our common faith (evangelization) and celebrate it (Eucharist).

During the Eucharist, we are not alone, but are connected with the believing community—some worshipping in majestic European cathedrals, others in simple, aboriginal churches—to remember and celebrate the eternal sacrifice of Jesus. We experience good news in action. Christ is truly present in the word, community, presider, and Eucharist (*The Constitution on the Sacred Liturgy*, #7).

Never before did I experience flesh and blood evangelization happening as it did with mom that morning. I realized that no true evangelization happens unless a Christian community celebrates it in the Eucharist. Here, the Eternal Word, first disclosed in creation, connects with that same Word-Made-Flesh, now present in word and sacrament. Furthermore, our Eucharistic experience connected with the missionary aspect of evangelization, for ". . . Evangelizing means bringing the Good News into all strata of humanity, and through its influence transforming humanity from within and making it new . . . " (EN, #18).

Faith

I wonder what a person, who came to our door and saw what was happening around the table, might have thought. Would the individual have thoughts of superstition, wonder, or ambiguity? The answer may depend on whether or not the person was a believer.

Even among believers, there may have been wonder. Without *faith*, what we celebrated around the table would make little sense. With faith, it made all the difference in the world. As I reflected with faith, I realized that it makes little essential difference *where* the liturgy is celebrated. But without faith, Eucharistic celebrations easily become rituals with little meaning, wherever they occur.

The Eucharist at the table celebrated our years together as a family. Evangelization demands faith, which inspires a Christian community to share its beliefs within the community itself and with the larger society. By its nature, evangelization demands outreach, for Jesus commanded the Church to "Go into all the world and proclaim the good news to the whole creation" (Mark 16:15).

The morning celebration touched us deeply because our family life had involved thousands of Eucharistic celebrations since childhood. We were at home with the ritual and our celebrating the Eucharist had deep meaning, because of our faith. This again indicates the connection between evangelization and Eucharist.

Christian faith invites us to search for life's meaning through a personal relationship with Jesus. On this journey, evangelization puts us in touch with the religious significance of our lives. Perhaps this is why our morning celebration of word and Eucharist, right after Dad's death, meant so much.

Ritual

Religious rituals are community celebrations of belief pattern or key life dimensions. They establish and maintain our identity, telling us who we are, how we are connected with a community, and how we fit into the larger world scheme. Rituals channel the emotional response which intellectual belief clarifies. In ritualizing transcendent reality, rituals make us feel at home in the world.

Without rituals, there is little core bonding or identity focus. Without rituals, there are few boundaries to channel powerful emotions, *especially our anger and fear*. Without rituals, there is no vehicle to celebrate deep feelings. Without rituals, there is no comfort level within which to develop creativity and meaningful goals. In life's struggles, rituals help us reinforce identity, when we hurt. They redirect identity, when we suffer loss. They restore identity, when we fail.

Contemporary society suffers from a disengagement of emotions because of a lack of significant rituals to channel them. Secular culture does not provide the deep rituals, which facilitate growth from childhood to maturity and from adulthood to old age. It does not help us cope ritualistically with strong emotions, like fear and anger. It disengages powerful life dynamics, like sexuality, from their *adequate moral expression* in friendship or marriage. Society's ritual patterns canonize superficiality, individualism, secularism, relativism, and materialism. Such inadequacies lead to meaninglessness and alienation, for they never reach life's core realities, like birth, suffering, death, happiness, identity, and the need to belong.

How different it was for Mom and me, as we celebrated the Eucharist! The Eucharist celebrated our core identity as individuals, family, and Catholics. During this trying time, it helped reinforce, redirect, and restore our identity, as we began to let go of my father, until eternity would reunite us.

The emotional bonding between Mom and me at the Eucharistic ritual was apparent. It reinforced a similar bonding with the larger faith community, especially our family and friends, as we gathered at St. Dominic Church to celebrate Dad's Mass of Christian Burial.

For Catholics committed to their faith, such bonding at a core level happens whenever the larger Church community gathers. Catholics, especially youth, often feel no emotional bonding with Church rituals, particularly the Eucharist. The challenge is to create opportunities for emotional bonding with a believing community itself, so that such bonding continues when the community gathers to worship. This presents a special challenge for an increasing number of Catholic mega-churches. Although the Mass is essentially the same, wherever it is celebrated, emotional bonding with community members affects its impact as a community action of evangelization and celebration.

When Catholics fail to connect with community rituals on a regular basis so that sacramental actions, especially the Eucharist, provide bonding with core Catholic beliefs, evangelization suffers. The *General Directory for Catechesis* states, "the proclamation of the Gospel and the Eucharist are the two pillars on which is built and around which gathers the particular Church" (GDC, #218).

When I reflect on that morning at the table, I remember my early years as a Catholic. My habits, sense of ritual, and psyche were honed by repeated sacramental rites that made me who I am today.

Today, I think of numerous children who do not attend Sunday Mass because it interferes with athletic or some other such activity. Parents, who attend these activities with their children and neglect Mass, discourage such sacramental ritual patterns. These actions do far more than parents imagine to shape the priorities, attitudes, and consciousness of their children. How can the good news be taken seriously when Sunday, a basic Christian sacred time, is minimized in favor of secular activities?

Eucharist

Evangelization's goal, the proclamation of the kingdom of God, culminates in the Eucharistic celebration of the death and resurrection of Jesus. The kingdom is fundamental, for "Christ first of all proclaims a kingdom, the kingdom of God; and this is so important that, by comparison, everything else becomes 'the rest', which is 'given in addition'" (EN, #8).

The Eucharist that Mom and I celebrated brought the kingdom to ritualistic fruition in its sacramental reenactment of the Paschal mystery. The kingdom's lived reality offers comfort in sorrow and joy in good times. The life-long character of evangelization allows various life experiences to provide new insights into the good news that we personally hear, share, and live. As we better understand evangelization, we better appreciate the Eucharist as the center and summit of the Church's life.

As I sat with Mom at the table, we celebrated key dimensions of the Eucharist. First and foremost, it is a profound act of *thanksgiving*, expressed by Jesus as he gave his life for us and made us participants in the world's ongoing salvation. Mom and I gave thanks for God's graciousness, manifested in the divine love that gave us Jesus as the reparation for our sins. We also gave thanks for Dad and united our life, (all joys and sufferings included) to Jesus' cross as our humble gift. Finally we thanked God for our family, friends, creation, and ourselves.

Secondly, thanksgiving leads to a better appreciation of the Eucharist as the *real presence* of the Lord among us. God's presence in nature and human life is brought to completion eucharistically in word and sacrament for "The mode of Christ's presence under the Eucharistic species is unique" (*Catechism of the Catholic Church*, #1374).

As in any meaningful symbol, such as a kiss or handshake, symbolic presence became real presence as the Risen Lord became one with Mom and me under the appearances of bread and wine. This presence brought to a climax the good news that we experienced in our daily lives.

Thirdly, the living presence of Christ in the body of the Church, represented by my mother and me, is complemented by his *sacrificial* presence at Mass. Jesus is the supreme sacrifice, and the Eucharist brings this ongoing salvific action alive in our midst. The *Rite of Christian Initiation of Adults* speaks of those about to celebrate the Sacraments of Initiation and underlines the significance of the Eucharist as a sacrifice in these words, "They are graced with adoption as children of God and are led by the Holy Spirit into the promised fullness of time begun in Christ and, as they share in the eucharistic sacrifice and meal, even to a foretaste of the kingdom of God" (RCIA, #206).

From this sacrificial dimension all other sacramental actions radiate. It is a reminder that the same Jesus, who once gave himself for us on the cross, continues to do so through his body, the Church, as we sacrifice for one another.

The sacrificial dimension of the Eucharist is challenged by a social climate where self-satisfaction rather than sacrifice rules the day. Even though we live in a land of affluence where few people lack the necessities of life, many suffer from alienation and loneliness. In reflecting on this condition, we conclude that a full human life requires discipline and sacrifice. This need to sacrifice connects with the eternal sacrifice of the cross. In uniting ourselves with Christ's sacrifice, we learn how sin brings unhappiness and sacrifice helps us discover our true identity.

Christian sacrifice brings evangelization to fruition, for Jesus says that if we wish to follow him, we must take up our cross. The Eucharist as sacrifice reminds us that we are sinners and need healing. We are Mary Magdalene, the paralytic, the Samaritan woman at the well, and the apostles who abandoned Jesus. The Eucharist reminds us that, like these first followers of Jesus, each of us will suffer, die, and be raised up to new life.

The Eucharist as sacrifice is the ritual that stands above all Christian rituals in promising us *hope*. No sin, no sickness, no disappointment, no pain keeps us from God's love and eventual liberation. The Eucharist celebrates our need to evangelize and be evangelized, for it promises peace on earth and eternal blessedness in heaven. This is why it is imperative for *all* evangelization to connect with the Eucharist. Every parish evangelization effort needs to regard evangelization and Eucharist as different sides of the same coin.

Many years have passed since Mom and I celebrated that Eucharist around our dining room table. As I reflect on evangelization and Eucharist, I remember the day after Mom spoke of the beautiful sun coming through her window. This time, I was with her. Following a ride to our Indiana farm house, Mom and I walked toward the car to return to Cincinnati. She stopped and said, "Bob, look at that sunset! It is even more beautiful than the one I described to you yesterday." As I looked at the sunset's beauty, I glanced at my mother's face. Seeing her beauty and the sunset's beauty, I thought, "If you and the sunset are so beautiful, how beautiful is God?"

Reflection Questions

Use the following questions to reflect privately on the importance of rituals and Eucharist in your life. If members of the group are comfortable in sharing with each other, they may want to communicate some of their reflections on these questions.

1. In whom have you witnessed Jesus this week?
2. "The family, like the Church, ought to be a place where the Gospel is transmitted and from which the Gospel radiates" (EN, #71). Reflect on how your family, in whatever way you define family, lives this quote, or could live it better.
3. What experience have you had that would have made no sense without faith?
4. Reflect on a time when you participated in a meaningful liturgy that was not held in a church? Why and how did this experience touch you or change you?
5. How does your example reflect the importance of Sunday Mass attendance?
6. What hope do you find in participating in the Eucharist?